■ TIANANMEN DIARY

ALSO BY HARRISON E. SALISBURY

Tiananmen Diary

■ THIRTEEN DAYS IN JUNE

Harrison E. Salisbury

Little, Brown and Company

BOSTON   TORONTO   LONDON

FIRST EDITION

Library of Congress Cataloging in Publication Data 89-85228

HC: 10 9 8 7 6 5 4 3 2 1
PB: 10 9 8 7 6 5 4 3 2 1

                    HC

Published simultaneously in Canada by
Little, Brown & Company (Canada) Limited

PRINTED IN THE UNITED STATES OF AMERICA

To the students of China and the people of Beijing who gave their lives for democracy in the days of Tiananmen.

Contents

Publisher's Note

In the study of history, we are taught to distinguish between primary and secondary documents, between voices that speak directly from their own experience and those that are filtered through another's memory or perceptions.

Through an astonishing coincidence, Harrison E. Salisbury has provided us with a firsthand account of the brutal massacre in Tiananmen Square, those days in June 1989 that shook the world. On assignment with a Japanese film crew making a documentary about the fortieth anniversary of the People's Republic of China, Salisbury found himself in a hotel room with a window on Tiananmen just as the student demonstrators and government troops slowly wheeled into position for their bloody confrontation.

The pages that follow record not only the terror and confusion in Beijing, but also the reaction in the countryside, where Salisbury traveled in the aftermath of the tragedy, and, later, his reflections on why and how it could have happened.

Acknowledgments

This diary would not have been possible without my assignment by Japan's NHK TV network to go to China to collaborate on a documentary marking forty years of the Chinese People's Republic. I want to acknowledge the wonderful assistance of NHK's film and production crew and that of many, many Chinese friends who tried their best, under severe handicaps, to assist in my understanding of what was happening in their country. And my hat is off to Roger Donald and the editorial and technical crew of Little, Brown, who have brought this book out with such skill and swiftness.

■ TIANANMEN DIARY

Day One
June 1, 1989

■ Aboard JAL Flight #5, New York–Tokyo,
6:00 P.M.

For thirty years I have been coming out to China but never at such a time. Students occupying Tiananmen Square. Chaos in the government. Future beclouded.

It is not only China. Now Marxist society — the Communist world that has been my beat since World War II — is dissolving before my eyes: Gorbachev in Russia, Deng in China, Poland turning to democratic elections, liberalization in Hungary. What next?

Beginning five years ago, when my wife, Charlotte, and I slogged seventy-four hundred miles through China's backcountry retracing the route of the Long March of Mao Zedong's Red Army in 1934–35, I have spent almost a third of my time in China.

I have traveled and interviewed relentlessly. There is hardly a single important Chinese political figure — except for Deng Xiaoping — whom I have not met. We have endlessly discussed where China is headed, where the great enlightenment that Deng has brought to his country is taking her.

Nor is there a corner of China from Tibet to the great Heilongjiang forests of the Soviet-Chinese border that I have not explored, hardly a city or a major industrial plant that I have not inspected. I think I know China as well as, if not better than, any member of the Standing Committee of the Politburo.

But I don't know what is happening now. Students have been demonstrating and sitting in Tiananmen Square since the death on April 15 of former party secretary Hu Yaobang. They are calling for democracy, an end to corruption among officials, an honest dialogue with the leaders.

The government has taken a harder and harder line since publication of an official declaration April 26 condemning the student demonstrations. Martial law was proclaimed May 19. Large numbers of troops are maneuvering in the city outskirts and deeper and deeper into the city itself.

What is going on in Zhongnanhai I cannot say. Zhongnanhai is the stately compound adjacent to the Forbidden City created as a pleasure park by the Ming and Ching dynasties. Since 1949 it has been the headquarters of the Chinese Communist party and the residence of most of its leaders.

It has been almost a year since I left China on my most recent trip, and I have been troubled since that time by a current in China's politics that I have not been able to grasp.

Deng's economic policies have invigorated China as never before, especially the countryside. Never have the peasants been so prosperous. But these policies have also stimulated inflation — estimated at 30 percent annually — creating a scissorslike squeeze on low-paid civil servants, notably in Beijing, who can't afford the high prices for food.

4

And there have been vast corruption and, I think, poor selection of foreign joint ventures, particularly with thieving Hong Kong partners — overbuilding of hotels and office buildings and other enterprises that make no contribution to China's technical and industrial growth.

But nothing, it seems to me, that could not be handled by a vigorous executive and a surer control of credit. Instead we have heard consistent offstage noises suggesting that something much more serious is wrong in China, something that would require the dumping of Deng's liberal program and a return, at least partially, to conventional Stalinist economic and social policy.

Now, unless I am mistaken, Party Secretary Zhao Ziyang — the leading liberal — has been thrown out in the crunch over a hard line on the students in Tiananmen Square. He hasn't been seen nor heard of since May 19, when he apologized to the students for being "too late, too late" in responding to their demands.

In his place have emerged the irritable figure of Premier Li Peng and the enigmatic one of General Yang Shangkun, president of China and a man I know very, very well.

Yang Shangkun supported the arrangements for my Long March expedition and subsequent book and was extremely helpful in my journeys in 1987 and 1988. What is he up to now? I wonder. I cabled him before leaving, saying I must see him at the earliest possible moment to discuss the current critical situation. And, once again, to ask to see Deng Xiaoping, the elusive little man. I told Yang I'd like to interview him and Li Peng on camera but that the only voice that had enough weight to get world attention was that of Deng Xiaoping. It's a long shot, but you don't get anything by not asking. No answer so far.

■ Tokyo, airport motel, 9:00 P.M.

This trip is different from all my others. In the early years when I first became fixated on the importance of the China story, I was an editor and reporter for the *New York Times*. Charlotte and I made a trip all around the edges of China in 1966, trying to figure out what was happening. At the end of twenty-five thousand miles we knew that a "Cultural Revolution" and some kind of power struggle were being waged by Mao. Not much else.

In later years I traveled on my own, always with some book assignment. Now I am going to China to finish work on a television documentary about the first forty years of the People's Republic. I am working with the Japanese TV network NHK. Junichi Takeda, NHK's New York correspondent, is traveling with me. An NHK film crew is already in China and has done considerable background filming. We hope to cover a lot of ground and interview many important figures in Beijing.

Whether the interviews will actually occur is another thing. One has been scheduled with Zhao Ziyang, whom I have gotten to know fairly well. I'm very dubious that this will come through. Or the one we have set up with Hu Qili, another member of the Politburo's Standing Committee, who disappeared along with Zhao.

Day Two
June 2, 1989

■ Aboard flight to Beijing, 2:00 P.M.

We took off at 1:00 P.M. Last night Takeda spoke with CCTV in Beijing: "The program is not yet arranged," they told him. Talked to Charlotte in Connecticut. Television reports that Beijing has issued a new warning to correspondents. Two or three have been called in by the Foreign Ministry. Several of Zhao Ziyang's aides have been arrested. General Yang Shangkun has issued a statement saying Zhao is suffering from a heart condition and dizzy spells. The People's Liberation Army troops are reportedly trying to get on a friendly basis with Beijing's citizens. There have been a couple of forays by armored columns into the city, but they have withdrawn.

What *is* going on? Before I left New York I telephoned an old friend in Beijing. He said: "You know more about it than we do." A Chinese friend in New York said he had talked to his relatives in Beijing (highly placed individuals). They spoke cautiously, as though afraid their line was tapped. He said he thought an army takeover was imminent.

We are walking into a volatile situation. Will people consent to be interviewed? Will they express themselves on camera? Not likely. Too dangerous. In phone conversations, a good many of my friends in China already were saying they supported the army. They told me that the

7

army didn't want to kill students and would not. "If one drop of blood is shed the government will fall." Another said that bloodshed would ruin China's international reputation. Yes, it would, but that reputation is already pretty well shot due to the equivocal way the government is acting. Would they bring troops into Beijing and not employ them? I think not.

■ Beijing Hotel, 4:40 P.M.

We got in at midafternoon. Airport almost empty. Streets much less crowded than usual. Hot day, 90 degrees at the airport. The JAL plane not very full. Chinese put the luggage through X-ray inspection *after* it had cleared customs! I guess the world here is upside down, as we had thought as children. NHK photographers taped me on the moving walkway after getting off the plane. Then made me do it again. I spoke my little homily — historic significance of the founding of the People's Republic, how Mao declared China had stood up, how Napoleon said that China was a sleeping giant and when she awoke she would shake the world. Is she awakening now? Or preparing for another long nap?

I was all eyes in the taxi, looking for signs of troop deployment. Saw none. The NHK crew said they had had to deal with the military to get permission to photograph me at the airport. I saw a lot of new planting along the highway, lovely flowers blazing in new beds. No troops hiding in the bushes.

The photographers wanted to go straight to Tiananmen. Then they changed their mind, because of the rule against picture taking. The traffic was light on Changan Avenue coming up to the Beijing Hotel. No military. The hotel is quite empty. Hardly any Americans, no Africans, a few Hong Kong tourists. Had an ice cream sundae while waiting to check in. Several Scandinavians in the lounge. I was given a ridiculously elaborate three-room suite on the seventh floor, on the Changan side. The only virtue is the view from the balcony up to Tiananmen.

So here I am in these plush surroundings. Waiting, I guess, for something to happen. No clear sense of what it might be. But that the city is pregnant with action I am convinced. You can almost feel it in the air. Everyone waiting — for what? I'll be here only a couple of days, in all probability, so I may miss it. Now I will start calling my friends and see what they think — whether I have come in time for the curtain to go up.

■ Beijing Hotel, 11:00 P.M.

I saw my friend Cui Lie this afternoon. Cui is with an international publishing and translation company, and he accompanied me in my 1987 and 1988 travels as I gathered materials for a book about the Deng regime, which I had tentatively titled *China's New Long March*. Somehow that doesn't seem quite appropriate today.

The Long March was translated and published in China by the Military Publishing House, in 1986, but Cui's firm won the rights to the new book. There is nothing for me in this, of course, since China does not belong to the international copyright convention. Cui's publishing house has also translated and has ready for publication, he told me, my book of memoirs called *A Time of Change*. That has a lot about China in it.

I had hoped that Zhang Yadong, the extremely

bright young Foreign Office interpreter who was with me last spring, could go on this mission, but he has been sent off to Europe by the Foreign Office and isn't available. But we have a fine young interpreter from CCTV, the Chinese TV network monopoly, which is coordinating our arrangements. She is Miss He, and she told me, "Call me Julie. That is my English name." So many young language students have picked up the old tradition of missionary days and given themselves "English" names that sound something like the Chinese equivalent.

A few people called me. Word does get around this town fast. One was the energetic Mr. Bao Shixiu of the Institute of Mao Zedong Military Thought. Ever since *The Long March* was published he has been trying to get me to lecture to his institute about Mao's tactics. I keep telling him that all I know is what Mao did on the Long March. That would be fine, he insists. Now he wants to talk about a trip he is making to the United States in a few days. He will drop by the hotel. I talked to my friend Dr. Grey Dimond of Kansas City, who is extremely well informed. We had a long chat before Bao came over. He is going down to Shanghai the day after tomorrow. He says the situation is exactly as we postulated in the States — difficult, dangerous, and ultimately to be resolved by the army and the security forces. A grim prospect. No mention of the "one drop of blood" hypothesis. I believe he expects brute force and then a quick and intensive roundup of students and intellectuals. Shades of the Cultural Revolution!

We went to a banquet at 6:00 P.M. given by Huang Haigun, CCTV's director, an intelligent, hardworking

10

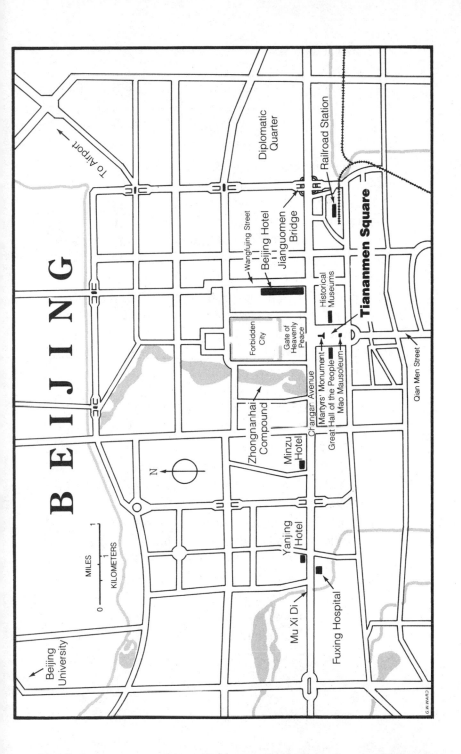

woman who knows her business and has been willing to stand up for the integrity of broadcasting insofar as she has been able. We were about forty minutes late because it took so long to pass through Tiananmen on the way to the Hunan restaurant near the CCTV building, where the banquet was held. At one hundred acres, Tiananmen is the largest public square in the world, bigger than Red Square, in Moscow, and St. Peter's, in Rome. It is bounded on the north by the Tiananmen Gate to the Forbidden City and the city itself. The New China Gate, at the northwest corner, leads to Zhongnanhai, the government compound. The east side is flanked by the Museum of History and the Museum of the Revolution. On the west is the Great Hall of the People. To the south are the remains of Qian Men, once the "front gate" to the Forbidden City. There are two structures within the square. One is the Monument to the Martyrs of the Revolution, an obelisk 120 feet high in front of the Tiananmen Gate. The memorial hall in which the embalmed body of Mao Zedong is kept on display is located almost at the center of the square, directly south of the martyrs' column.

Normally traffic flows through the square along the north side, adjacent to the Forbidden City walls. But just two lanes were open and the jam of buses was so great I caught only occasional glimpses of the square. I was surprised to see so few students there, seemingly lost in the vast stone expanse. Most of them were in front of the Great Hall of the People or clustered between the Martyrs' Monument and the Mao mausoleum.

A lively dinner with lots of talk about *The Yellow River Elegy,* an extraordinary political-historical documentary that CCTV showed last summer. It challenges all the key, established myths in China's ideology. The reactionaries tried to suppress it, but Zhao Ziyang ordered it aired a second time. I can't believe Deng Xiaoping liked it very much.

One of *Yellow River*'s directors was there and told me that he and his colleagues had projected a second documentary about the May Fourth students' movement of 1919, which is the direct ancestor of the demonstration on Tiananmen, but did not receive government permission. I think it will be a long, long time coming, even though some of those in the government participated in the December 9, 1934, students' movement and have always hallowed the name of the May Fourth students. But that, I am afraid, is in the great Communist tradition of honoring dead, not living, heroes.

No one has a clue as to how to get out of this jam. Our CCTV hostess told me she thought the government "has displayed remarkable tolerance. Not one student has been arrested." The only people arrested, she said, were eleven motorbikers who had roared around town, creating a lot of noise and disturbing people, and they had only just been taken into custody. In fact, they were couriers and scouts who alerted the people if troops were coming. Their arrest deprived the demonstrators of their Paul Reveres. I did think the government had been tolerant. Almost quizzically tolerant, but I was suspicious that this tolerance was the velvet that conceals the mailed fist.

None of this speculation solved the basic problem. How had the standoff between the students and the government come about? Some were saying it had been caused by a split in the government and its subsequent indecision. People said that Zhao Ziyang opposed force as a solution.

Before his recent fall from favor, Zhao had been known as an old political hand, a man who knew how to get things done, even over the heads of his nominal superiors. Zhao, I remarked to the company at the banquet, had been party secretary for Sichuan, a wheat-growing region, hadn't he, and had done well there. I then quoted a couplet that I knew had been circulated all over China. (I had quoted it to Zhao himself when I dined with him a couple of days after he was named party secretary at the Thirteenth Party Congress, in November 1987.) The couplet named both Zhao and Wan Li, now president of the People's Congress and former party secretary of Anhwei, a rice-growing region. "If you want wheat you go to Zhao Ziyang," the couplet ran, "if you want rice you go to Wan Li." Everyone chuckled, for they remembered that these two once-powerful men had kept their provinces from starvation. Of course everyone knew that Zhao was now in bad trouble. I was certain he would be dismissed as party secretary and possibly suffer worse punishment. As for Wan Li, he had been in the United States when the trouble broke out and was detained when he returned for being sympathetic to the students.

We came back through Tiananmen at about 8:30 P.M. The traffic had thinned and I had a better look. Many more people in the square and lots of young people on bicycles making their way there. There were clusters all over the square. Very lively. Many had been drawn

14

out by the appearance of the Taiwanese rock star Hou Dejian, who had joined in with three Beijing intellectuals in a hunger strike. He was sitting with his companions, cross-legged, and singing numbers from his repertoire.

The tent colony was neat, almost military in the way it was laid out, and the Goddess of Freedom — the students' symbol of liberty — loomed high. It was placed rather deep in the center of the square, not just below the famous picture of Mao, as it had seemed in the TV shots.

There was nothing tense about the mood at Tiananmen as darkness began to thicken; instead, it seemed to me rather a holiday atmosphere. Young people hanging out, aimless sightseeing. Going to Tiananmen is the *in* thing. Lots of people, I was told, drop in every evening on the way home from work, just checking to see that it is still there.

When my Japanese colleagues and I got back to the hotel, we sat in my lavish suite and discussed our plans. We are spending tomorrow, Saturday, June 3, here in Beijing. A free day. On Sunday, June 4, we will visit the Military Museum in the morning. I look forward to that. I will see my old friend General Qin Xinghan, who was my companion on the Long March. He is director of the museum, and I am very fond of him, as is Charlotte. He is a wonderful officer, a good historian, and a fabulous singer of Beijing Opera songs.

We leave Monday for Wuhan, spend a couple of days there, then travel by steamboat on the Yangtze east to Jiujiang, a small river port about a hundred miles from Shanghai. There we'll take a minibus up Mount Lu, an old missionary summer resort where Mao kicked off the preliminaries to the Cultural Revolution by firing his right-hand general, Peng Dehuai. Then south to Nanchang to have a look at the place where Deng Xiaoping was confined under house arrest for three and a half years during the Cultural Revolution. Finally on to Changsha and Shaoshan to see the homes of Mao Zedong; Liu Shaoqi, the martyred president of the People's Republic; and Peng Dehuai, who eventually succumbed to Mao's torturers. When we get back to Beijing we hope to interview some of the important people we had lined up before the crisis.

All of this subject to change without notice. There is one serious problem. We had planned to do a lot of filming around Tiananmen and in the leadership compound of Zhongnanhai. For the present that is out. No photography permitted. But since what we want is Tiananmen Gate as a backdrop for some of my essays, we could easily shoot it early in the morning. There is no activity around the gate then, and we could get in and out without attracting attention. This would require special permission from the military. No reason for them to object — under present conditions. But knowing the military, that doesn't mean that we can get the permission. We will see.

Just before going to bed I called Charlotte in Connecticut. She told me Ross Terrill, a colleague and author of several books about China, had phoned. He will be here tomorrow. "I just can't not be there," he told Charlotte. I may miss him, depending on whether we leave tomorrow, Sunday, or Monday.

Day Three
June 3, 1989

■ Beijing Hotel, 2:00 P.M.

I had slept soundly but I started awake at 5:00 A.M. Very quiet. Too quiet. Looked out the window. No traffic on Changan. I've had rooms on Changan before. Seemed to me there was always action on the street. Odd. After an hour and still not a car or bus had passed, I decided to have a look. I got out a little before 7:00 A.M. There were pedicabs at the hotel gate. All wanted to take me up to the square. I guess they are doing a good business. Hardly any taxis. Drivers, I was told, are afraid their cars will be seized by the demonstrators and piled up onto the barricades.

Nothing but bicycles and pedestrians on Changan. I strolled up toward the square, a couple of blocks to the west. My eyes were alert for anything that might tell me what had happened during the night. There were many knots of older people discussing something, particularly at the corner of Nanheyan Street, which forms the western boundary of the Beijing Hotel area and where its new tower addition is going up. This is a quiet, old-fashioned street. A few steps from the corner is a pleasant court-yard where the Returned Foreign Students Club (dating back to the 1920s or earlier) has its quarters; a room or two houses the Gung Ho Society, founded in the 1930s by Edgar Snow and Rewi Alley to foster cooperatives in China.

All traffic was halted at this intersection. A bus with slashed tires was slanted in front of the Beijing Hotel, and an elephant's tail of four connected buses blocked the crossroads. Bikes and pedestrians could just squeeze by. The barricade of buses, I thought, was the modern equivalent of the heaped-up paving stones of the French Revolution.

Just entering the square as I arrived was a band of forty young people, hoisting a big red flag, reinforcements for their comrades in the square. As I left the hotel I had heard several choruses of cheers. Probably for the arrival of this and other new units. Judging by the demeanor of the little chatting groups, I had the feeling that the students must have won some battles during the night.

At the square itself I found another barricade to traffic. I skirted this by walking along a sidewalk next to some shrubbery beside the bleachers from which invited spectators view the anniversary parades of May 1 and October 1. There was a morning breeze, and the air for once in Beijing smelled fresh and not laden with yellow dust from the Gobi.

As the square opened up before me I could see that the students occupied only a quarter of its expanse. On the Tiananmen Gate side three traffic lanes were left open for bicycles, buses, and cars. There is a broad sidewalk here and two pedestrian underpasses coming up on the edge of the square proper. The student occupation seemed to start at the Martyrs' Column, directly in front of Tiananmen Gate. The column is a blocky, rather unattractive granite obelisk that Mao put up in 1958 to honor the heroes of the Revolution. It stands on a double pediment that provides a kind of platform, which had been turned into a permanent forum from which students addressed the throngs, speaking through bullhorns. Around the base of the column are bas-reliefs depicting scenes from China's Revolution, one of them illustrating the students' movement of 1919, the famous May Fourth movement. The seventieth anniversary of this predecessor of today's movement had been celebrated by the students with a huge gathering around the column.

Just to the south was the large permanent camp, neat military rows of olive-drab nylon tents donated from Hong Kong. Here was the command post and here in the center rose the Goddess of Freedom, stark and white.

The area around the Mao mausoleum and the northern outskirts of the square were almost empty. Only when huge throngs of demonstrators appeared was the whole vastness of the square filled.

I saw at the far western edge of the square another blockade. No wonder no traffic was flowing on Changan Avenue. It would not be easy, I thought, even for a tank to make its way through these tangles of buses and overturned automobiles. But there was little in the scene to arouse apprehension.

A beggar, a legless cripple, sat on the sidewalk with a big sign beside him. I suppose it was a plea for help, but no one was interested. People were strolling casually, munching their breakfast buns. Here and there a harassed-looking bureaucrat, briefcase in hand, was hurrying to his office, no doubt cursing the lack of buses and the demonstrators. There were young people who seemed to wander about. They could have been scouts, watching out for enemy threats. Or just demonstrators getting the kinks out of their muscles after a night on the pavement. In the bushes I saw several old people squatting and staring into space. Also a few persons stretched out, not yet awake after a night in the open.

For the first time I had a good look at the Goddess of Freedom, still standing, made of plastic and not very beautiful. The students had put it up three days ago. I had thought that during the night there might have been a battle over the statue. But that was not the case. The students' placement of the statue in the square had irritated the authorities more than any other of their actions. You could feel their outrage in every statement made about it on TV and in the papers. Yet there was the goddess, just as she had been the night before. I thought of Francis Scott Key and the Star-Spangled Banner, still flying "by dawn's early light."

I thought to myself, Here I am again in a place where a reporter discovers what is happening by using his eyes, his ears, and his nose. You walked to the scene and looked — intently. No handouts. Sometimes there was news in the *People's Daily*, the party paper, sometimes not. The best was *Youth Daily*, the Young Communist paper. The reporters and editors on its staff were bubbling with eagerness to report what was happening. But all depended on the censors. The same with Beijing TV — good reporters, often Western-trained, covering the news, trying to report it as it was. But the dead hand of the party controlled the switches. Some days and in some editions amazingly frank truths blazoned forth.

Other days, other editions, just gray propaganda. The principal source of news for the Beijinger was just what it had been a hundred, two hundred, or three hundred years ago — word of mouth, what used to be called the bazaar telegraph. Fast, exciting, forever erring on the side of exaggeration and wishful thinking.

As I stood staring at the scene a couple of young men took up their powerful loudspeakers and began to harangue the sparse crowd. What they were saying I could not guess. Once again, as at so many times in China, I wished that I had had sense enough to learn the language so that I would not forever be having to depend on an interpreter or asking someone what was going on. No one seemed to pay attention to the speech. I stood for quite a time staring at the great portrait of Mao at the Tiananmen Gate. It had been defaced a week or so earlier by young men who the students swore were provocateurs, and now it had been replaced by an identical twin. I guessed there were plenty more in the warehouses, for nothing had been less rare in the days when I first came to Beijing. Now Mao portraits and statues were hard to find, and the Little Red Book of his sayings had vanished completely.

People were going in and out of the main entrance to the Forbidden City. They were workers in the enclave, clerks, service personnel. There must be hundreds or thousands on the Forbidden City payroll.

All was quiet at the Gate of Heavenly Peace when I saw a young man run like a deer from the encampment on the square, vault over a low fence, and plunge across the marble bridge and into the Forbidden City. Within a

21

minute young men were running or cycling from all directions and tearing toward the entrance passage. I crossed the bridge and tagged along after them. Before I could get more than a few paces inside they began to stream back. False alarm.

I sauntered out and stood on the marble bridge looking down at the Golden River, as is called the little stream that flows along the city's perimeter. This was where the family of Liu Shaoqi, former president of China who had been murdered on Mao's orders, scattered his ashes. In his last meeting with his family Liu had said he wanted his ashes tossed into the sea, like those of Friedrich Engels. But his wife cried: "Suppose they won't give them to us?" "They will," Liu said confidently. It took his children six years to locate an unmarked urn they believed held his ashes. Just before October 1, 1976, they threw his remains into the Golden River, which, they thought, would eventually take them to the sea. Mao had died in September, and the fall of the Gang of Four was at hand. Never again, everyone said, would China suffer such a period of madness, death, and repression. Never again, people said, and rallied around Deng Xiaoping, himself a victim of the Cultural Revolution, who took the same pledge against a new reign of terror.

Finally I pushed these thoughts from my mind and turned back toward the hotel. I was almost out of the square when I bumped into a tall, thin Englishman in his early thirties. He recognized me. I think he was a Reuters correspondent. He had been in and out of the square all night and had not lost his excitement. He told me what he thought had happened. About 2:00 A.M. two or more

22

bodies of troops had approached Tiananmen from different directions.

Those coming from the east were on foot, marching up the street unarmed. They did not seem to be a very formidable body. They had been surrounded by ordinary citizens as they approached the square and (as it later became clear) had turned back in the direction from which they had come in a state of some bewilderment.

A second column, from the west, was more impressive. It consisted mostly of troops in trucks escorting more troops in buses. The truck troops apparently were not armed. Those in the buses were. The motorized outfit had moved at a fairly rapid pace and without opposition until an accident occurred. A truck hit some civilians and, the English reporter thought, two people had been killed, possibly more. The students said four were dead.

The accident gave the students time to spread the alarm, and citizens swarmed out and surrounded that column as well. These troops also retreated, after some angry shouting. The people the Reuters man had talked to described the troops as being dispirited. Some said they thought they had been going to the railroad station (not far away, on the eastern approaches to the square). Others thought they were on "night maneuvers." They didn't know anything about the students, the demonstration, or what was going on in Beijing. No one had told them.

The Reuters man excused himself and hurried on through the crowd. There was a rumor that the students had captured a general in plain clothes who was making a reconnaissance of the square and were holding him hostage. He had to get to the west side of the square and check it out. [So far as I ever heard there was no basis for the rumor.]

I made my way back to the hotel with some difficulty. There was a very narrow path past the roadblocks and hundreds of people with their bikes trying to get past. The sidewalk at the corner of the new Beijing Hotel tower was torn up, and people were sliding and slipping along it. Just ahead of me was an elderly cripple with two canes, pushing ahead at a steady pace. No one made way for him. He slipped at one point, and I helped him to his feet. No one else paid him any attention. So I did my good deed for the day.

As I came up to the Beijing Hotel I ran into a young man who said he was with CNN. Very excited with the story. Thousands of troops had been moving all night long. They were in motion in all different directions. All of them, he said, had been brought to a halt by the people who swarmed into the streets. I asked how they were getting pictures out. He told me that they were breaking down the videotape frame by frame and in some fashion could send it out on ordinary phone lines as individual pictures; then the pictures were reconstituted in New York as film. He was full of the technology of it, but I don't know enough to understand. I do know, however, that Beijing, amazingly, had a very high-tech communications system and even the shutting off of the satellite hasn't kept the media from getting their stuff out, one way or another, much of it being couriered to Tokyo.

Inside, the hotel was gloomy and empty. Just about vacant. The young CNN man told me to come up to the

CNN office, on the fourteenth floor. They could offer a great view up to the square and maybe even a Coke. He then ran off on another mission.

I had a date with a couple of Chinese friends for an 8:00 A.M. breakfast. But they didn't appear. Finally I sat down in the almost empty Western-style dining room. This had been the main dining room of the Beijing Hotel in the days when Mao took over. The first diplomatic reception in the People's Republic of China was held here, to celebrate India's national day, a great event. Mao attended and made a speech. "The Indian nation is a great nation," he said.

On this morning it was grim. The hostesses with their magenta dresses and slit skirts had nothing to do. Even the busboys were quiet. No giggling. No horseplay. I sat down with my NHK colleagues and had breakfast. My friends, I guessed, hadn't been able to make it. But I was wrong. They appeared about 9:00 A.M., apologetic. They had biked it and had, I think, to walk the last part of the way to the hotel.

"What's happening?" I asked. "We don't know," they said. "It's very confusing. The troops have taken over the railroad station."

I said I had understood the railroad station had been jammed with troops for a couple of days. "Is the political situation just as confused?"

They nodded in agreement. Some rumors, they said, were that Deng Xiaoping had been isolated and that he had little influence on what was happening. It was their guess that Yang Shangkun, the president, was acting as the operational chief and that Premier Li Peng was only a front man for Chen Yun, the eighty-three-year-old conservative.

I had last seen Chen Yun in November 1987, at the Thirteenth Party Congress. He had been so ill and feeble he had been unable to sit through a session. He did not appear at all at the next session. It was hard to believe he had mustered enough energy and allies to take over from Deng. But my friends seemed confident that this was indeed true, and I knew they were well informed. The country, they thought, was in the hands of five old men headed by Chen Yun, and it was moving toward a terrible economic collapse. The five old men, they thought, had no idea of a solution for the crisis. My friends' words were permeated with gloom and doom.

We had a cup of coffee and some croissants (I wondered if the croissants were a delicate tribute to Deng Xiaoping, who had acquired a taste for them when he lived in France as a work-study student and was so short of money he lived on a croissant and a glass of milk a day). We agreed to meet again but probably not until I returned to town, since I was hoping to leave on Monday for ten days in the country.

A bit later another Chinese friend dropped by. He had also come by bicycle, and I suddenly realized that the buses weren't running. I had heard that the drivers didn't like going out on the streets because the demonstrators were likely to seize the buses and use them for barricades; the taxis had almost vanished for the same reason. My friend said he had been awakened about 2:00 A.M. by shouts in his street of "The troops are coming!

26

The troops are coming!" He got up and dressed and went out into the street to join hundreds of his neighbors. Together they had barred the troops from the street. The crowd halted their trucks and surrounded them and persuaded them to turn back.

These troops, like so many of whom I had heard, were young, inexperienced, and totally ignorant of what was happening in Beijing. I had yet to meet or hear of anyone who was not totally sympathetic to the students. Many, I knew, were very angry with the government — not about the troops and the demonstrations but about the terrible inflation. A lot of Beijingers simply could no longer afford to buy their normal food supplies. The reports and rumors of scandals, bribe taking, graft, and corruption by top party leaders had made them even more angry, and they vented their rage by supporting the student demonstrations and blocking the path of the troops.

My friend was hoping to go abroad in a few weeks on a government mission and would have to leave his family behind. In spite of all the problems he didn't seem depressed.

I went back to my room and listened to a BBC broadcast. There had been some fighting between troops and the students in or around Tiananmen Square. That was new. So far as I had heard there hadn't been anything like that before. Also there was another report, about an army column that had been halted by a car crash as it was rolling into the city. It was supposed to involve a camera crew on a truck. Whether it was an army camera crew or civilian wasn't specified. Many people think there could be a general showdown tonight. I haven't got a feeling about that. Haven't been here long enough to feel clued in, although it was hard to believe last night with the rock music and sightseers that danger was imminent. I was tired and after lunch in the Chinese dining room took a little nap. I had had my favorite Beijing lunch — plain noodles with little chicken slices, and some crispy chicken. Good, but I didn't think the noodles quite as succulent as I remembered them last year.

■ Beijing Hotel, 10:00 P.M.

About six o'clock Junichi Takeda and my Japanese camera crew came by, and we decided to go over to the square. They wanted to take some still pictures of me. They had been at Tiananmen earlier, looking for suitable sites. Actually, we wanted to do a good deal of filming in the square, especially up around Tiananmen Gate, and we hoped to get permission for me to stand up on the balcony where Mao stood when he proclaimed the People's Republic on October 1, 1949, and where he had stood during all the great demonstrations of the Cultural Revolution, waving and occasionally speaking a bit to throngs of one million or more, most of them his chosen Red Guards, the ones who carried out most of the atrocities against his former henchmen and the population in general.

I was agreeable. I hadn't really gotten the feel of the square in my morning visit. It was still hot, the sun shining down, but not as hot as yesterday. My friends didn't take any television cameras, because they were barred by the rules, and with all the taping we had to do they didn't want to get into trouble.

We strolled down Changan toward the square, and I was glad to see that the huge jam that had blocked the corner at the end of the hotel compound with the tower had dissipated. My friend Takeo Iida, the little photographer with a great head of black bobbed hair, was in his glory because he had all these new backgrounds against which to snap still pictures of me.

It was good to be out of the sour atmosphere of the Beijing, vacant, many of its shops closed, lights turned off in some of the corridors. Already the hotel employees were failing to attend to business. The daily papers in the newsstand were just tossed on the inner counter instead of in the neat piles I was accustomed to. Of course, there was no one there to buy or read the *Herald-Tribune* or the *South China Morning Post,* so why bother? The clerks stood in little huddles talking quietly. None of the gay shouting across the room.

In the hotel shop, usually crowded, especially with Hong Kong visitors, where they sell cashmere sweaters, I found emptiness and a single young boy to wait on the trade. I bought a lovely pink cardigan for Charlotte. There were stacks of them. Ordinarily they never have more than one or two and never in the style or color you want. The young man knew no English, but we made out somehow.

There didn't seem much tension in the air, or at least my nerves relaxed as we walked along. There were lots of people just strolling in the late afternoon sunshine. We had almost got to the edge of the square when I bumped into Bill Hinton, looking as much like a farmer as you could imagine, an old-fashioned American farmer's hat on his head to shield his red face from the sun. I almost expected to see a fresh wheat straw sticking between his buck teeth as he walked along with a slow farmer's roll. There wasn't an American living, I supposed, who knew China better. Bill had lived in China for years. He came from a missionary family, and he had been sympathetic to the efforts of the Communists to get their agriculture going. He had written the classic book on Communism in the Chinese countryside, *Fanshen,* the story of the village where he had lived and worked. He spent part of every year in China advising farm organizations on agricultural practices and part of the year running his own farm in Pennsylvania.

With Bill was Nick Kristoff, the bright young *New York Times* man who had gotten into China with his new bride only a few months ago, just in time to handle the biggest China story in years — and handle it wonderfully well. He had spent a lot of time in Hong Kong, knew the language, and was off and running the moment he hit the ground in Beijing.

He and Bill had come from the west end of the square, where, as I learned, there had been a lot of action, two big encounters between students and troops, more serious than any that had come before. One confrontation had happened in the little street just behind the Great Hall of the People. Neither Bill nor I knew its name. There had been scuffling and fighting back and forth, and finally the troops had been forced back into the Great Hall. The second fight was apparently the same one I had already heard about, in which a detachment of the 8341 security regiment, the top outfit that protects Zhongnanhai and the leadership group, had swarmed out of the New China Gate and attacked students who had surrounded a couple of busloads of officers. The 8341 unit, using tear gas and batons, had quickly and easily rescued the two buses and brought the officers into Zhongnanhai through the New China Gate. Gas, I knew, had not been used before in this conflict. This was its first use since the demonstration had begun, in April. It seemed surprising to me that this top security group would emerge from Zhongnanhai with all the other troops that were now deployed right around the square, but I had already concluded that the military operations had not been conducted according to what I would have considered sound military or riot-control principles. There was a curious sense of ad hoc decisions and operations that seemed part of some hidden agenda, one not necessarily related to the student encampment in the square.

Bill had decided to get away from the gas and had moved east across the square. I thought he was a bit sheepish at being chased out of the square by the threat of tear gas, but in any event the day was coming to an end. He was on his way to visit his sister, who had a place in Beijing. We agreed that we would try to get together in the next two or three days before I left town. I told Bill that he should call me at the Beijing Hotel and that if we missed each other we'd get together when I got back to Beijing, about June 20. We joked about the strange places we tended to bump into each other. The

31

last time had been four years earlier, when I walked out of the lovely old courtyard house that had belonged to Kang Sheng, Mao's sinister secret police operative. It was now a rather exclusive and pleasant small hotel called the Bamboo Gardens. I had been attending a writers' meeting and Bill, as usual, had just finished an assignment, giving advice to a cattle-breeding ranch in Inner Mongolia.

I walked on into the square. I was heading for the Tiananmen Gate to check out again my theory that we could come into the square in early morning and shoot our sequences without disturbing the demonstrators or the peace, but my Japanese photographer, Mr. Iida, wanted some pictures in the encampment, so we ducked down the underpass that leads from one side of Changan into the square.

It's a rather wide underpass, and on the side walls were many posters and notices; some were just names of people who had been there, others were declarations, some notes to friends telling where others could be found, the kind of bulletin board we often saw at demonstrations in the United States in the sixties, particularly during sit-ins, which this Chinese occupation so strongly resembled.

In fact, I think one reason it won instant recognition in the United States was that, in a sense, it was nostalgic. Not just of the Berkeley or Columbia sit-ins, but the whole protest period. True, these were Chinese youngsters and they had sweatbands on their foreheads with strange Chinese characters in red and black, but we could see our own students, our own youth, and our own protests. They even, I was told, sang some songs from the sixties, and "We Shall Overcome" was often sung in English by people who did not comprehend the specific words but understood the song's meaning.

There was another, not so pleasant analogy, I thought. The underpass reminded me too much of Grand Central and the homeless bedded down for the night in similar underpasses. There were a goodly number of people asleep against the walls, usually with a backpack for a pillow, some with blankets, some with padded cotton quilts, some with nothing. Some of them looked ill, almost as if they were running a high fever, but that may have been my imagination. The tunnel was not brightly lighted, and it had a bit of the fetid odor of which I had heard in connection with the square (but did not experience when I came out on the pavement).

As we came up from the underpass I could see that there were a good many young people moving around, chatting and, as I imagined, exchanging experiences. Some were obviously visitors, some probably the veterans who had been on the pavement for weeks. It was Woodstock, I guess, without drugs and certainly not as many people at 6:30 or 7:00 in the evening of June 3.

We went over to the Martyrs' Column. Now standing in the declining sunshine, I listened to a student speaking through a bullhorn. I was surprised at the strength of the horn. I had read that the government loudspeakers around the square were so strong they drowned out the student calls. I didn't see how that was possible with the volume these horns were throwing out.

No one seemed to be paying any attention to the

message being delivered through the horns. I suspected that the speakers had repeated themselves so often that the words flowed over the heads of the crowd without making much impression.

Tiananmen had become a must item for tourists, and many were in the square. I overheard four or five from the Midwest, easily recognizable by their flat accents, from St. Louis or Indianapolis, I thought, two men in sports shirts and three women in rather summery light dresses. They seemed to be in their seventies. Probably from one of the package tours that preoccupy so much time of American middle-class retirees.

They were talking avidly with some of the young people, using an interpreter, a young man who probably was with the tour group. I noticed a middle-aged woman and her husband, she with a broad-brimmed hat, he with a sunshade. They were from the South, Georgia or North Carolina, I guessed. They were asking a couple of young men where they were from, what college, what city, what they had been studying, how long they had been on the square.

I spotted quite a few folks from Hong Kong, the girls in white summer bonnets seemingly made of that spun sugar that adorns birthday cakes and wearing dresses of white crepe de chine. They had walked right out of 1922. They were flirting with some young demonstrators in white shirts and summer tans. These boys were quite well dressed but had a faint, faraway expression in their eyes that I saw on a good many faces, as though only part of their mind was with the visitors in the square, the other half in some distant zone where, at any moment, bullets might spurt out and death be at hand.

34

Somehow I found myself talking with a young man from Lanzhou who had been in the square for about a week and then another from, I think, Guiyang. Suddenly, one of the students recognized me. Not hard to do. A tall, white-haired, blue-eyed man. Many people in China recognize me because they have read my book on the Long March, which became a best-seller. Only about six weeks ago one of my Chinese friends had sent me a clipping about a poll of 250,000 college students who had picked *The Long March* as the best book published in the last ten years. So several of them pulled out notebooks or scraps of paper and wanted me to autograph them. I suppose I must have signed my name half a dozen times or more: "Harrison E. Salisbury, Tiananmen, June 3, 1989."

They were all so young and, when they found out who I was, so eager to come up and get an autograph. Several asked me if I was going to write about the square and the demonstration, and I said I was. "Tell the truth," one of them said. I told him I would try. I didn't bother to jot down where they were all from. I should have.

One boy, a brown plastic bag over his shoulder, joined the circle that formed around me. He spoke fairly good English. He had arrived that afternoon on the train from Tianjin, where he was a student at Nankai University. "Oh!" I told him I had been there just a year before. Nankai is a famous university and was established, along with a high school, with American funding after the Boxer Rebellion of 1900, I think, with some of the funds of the Boxer indemnity — the financial penalty imposed by the Western powers after they had crushed the Boxers. The United States had returned its share of the money to China for use in education and health. Nankai is one of China's top universities, and its high school is among the best half-dozen in the country. It has many famous graduates. Zhou Enlai attended, and his math teacher had been the mother of John Hersey, the writer. John liked to joke that he had attended school with Zhou, since his mother was pregnant with him at the time Zhou was studying there. Besides Nankai University, Tianjin has several other institutions of higher education and was well represented in Tiananmen's student encampment.

The young man's eyes glowed with happiness at the talk about his school. "Are you a demonstrator?" I asked.

"No," he said, "but I am a supporter."

"Well, so am I," I said. "It's a good cause."

I didn't think to ask the young man whether his school still observed the rules that I had seen posted there, dating from before the time of Zhou Enlai and John Hersey. I had jotted down an English translation of "The Nankai Creed":

> Face clean, hair cut,
> Clothes neat and buttoned up.
>
> Posture proper, shoulders square,
> Chest out and back held straight.
>
> Arrogance, hot temper, idleness,
> Always guarded against.
>
> Friendliness, composure, dignity,
> Sought for with every effort.

Those were the high school rules. Perhaps they didn't apply in the university, but they seemed to be embodied in the bright face and friendly smile of the young man. He wasn't wearing a jacket, but his clothes were neat and his hair cut. I didn't think he would have any trouble making it at Amherst, say, or Swarthmore. He was very happy to be with the students in the square and very happy that he had met me. He had read *The Long March*. It had told him, he said, so many things he had never known before about the march and about the leaders, Mao and the rest. There wasn't any Chinese book that dealt with them as real people.

I said good-bye to the group of students and wandered into the students' permanent camp and its cluster of nylon half-moon tents. As I walked through the tents there were, here and there, neat flattened heaps where the remains of earlier and more primitive shelters had been squashed down. I smelled no garbage, although my Japanese friends had mentioned this after visiting the square the night before. Perhaps it was because of a breeze that seemed to blow gently across the great stone expanse.

I noticed that there were quite a few people sleeping in the tents. I was surprised at first; then I realized that most of the action at Tiananmen was at night. Most people, I thought, probably were up all night. A quiet, early Saturday evening was a good moment to catch up on sleep. The boys outnumbered the girls at least three or four to one. I suppose there were older students, but the average age looked like twenty-five.

Here in the heart of the encampment the mood

seemed purposeful. The olive-drab tents were neatly placed in horizontal patterns, and in the center of the hollow square were massed colors. Over each tent a carefully lettered sign proclaimed the origin of each contingent. There were delegations from all over China, from all the prestigious universities, like Fudan in Shanghai, Xinghua in Beijing, and People's University in Beijing, the big institutes of physics, engineering, medical studies, electric power, and science.

Here and there on the pavement were soda and popsicle vendors, giving the scene a little of the atmosphere of a small-town summer festival.

We went over to the side of the encampment facing the Great Hall of the People. There was a row of silent soldiers sitting on the top step of the entrance across the street. It looked as though several rows of tents along this side of the quadrangle had been abandoned, the canvas and plastic collapsed on the pavement, resembling the skins of some animals of a future age. Probably they had left the row when the new, more commodious, and waterproof Hong Kong tents were brought in. We went back to the Martyrs' Column with its low barricade setting the space off from the general area of the square. A student was talking — actually two students were talking, facing in opposite directions with their bullhorns. I heard what I thought was someone issuing a warning of some kind. It wasn't. It was just a student making an announcement. Someone was coming to speak at 8:00 P.M. I peeped into some more of the tents. Again I was surprised to find so many asleep, exhausted by the night alarms, the heavy routine. What would they awaken to?

I guess the key positions in the square are the small area around the Martyrs' Monument and a clearing around the Goddess of Freedom, in the middle of the square. I am afraid neither monument nor statue is a thing of great beauty, but that really doesn't matter.

The tourists and visitors passed easily and freely through the encampment. I didn't see any security by the students. No problem for the government to send in spies or provocateurs if they wanted to, but I've not heard of much activity like that. I wanted to go over to the New China Gate again and have a look at the pro forma picket line I had noticed earlier.

I have been doing a lot of study lately on Zhongnan-hai and the palace where Mao Zedong lived. It was called the Study of Chrysanthemum Fragrance, and it is located just behind that gate. The gate itself is never used for visitors. One enters from Number 81 Nanchang Street, at the side or from the back of the compound through Beihai Park.

Actually, the "New China" Gate was given that name only after the Chinese Republic was set up in 1911. Before that it was a tower that Emperor Qian Long built for his favorite, the Fragrant Concubine. I doubt if the stone-faced guards of Security Regiment 8341 or the half-dozen pickets standing in front of the red enamel pillars have any idea of who the Fragrant Concubine was or that she used to climb this tower to look over the wall at the Moslem mosque and settlement just beyond.

In those days it was known as the Tower of Yearning. I guess Mao would have known that history. Despite all his campaigns against the "Four Olds" in the Cultural

Revolution, Mao was an addict of Chinese legend. But he didn't pass much of that on to the next generation.

By this time my Japanese friends had taken thirty or forty snapshots of me and were ready to go, so we crossed the massive stone square, ducked again into the underpass, a bit more sinister now with the light beginning to fade, and made our way along the rows of bleachers, across the little park, and back to the hotel.

I had planned to have dinner with my Japanese colleagues in the seventh-floor dining room, the old Tan family restaurant that Zhou Enlai persuaded to move into the hotel from Qian Men, the old South Gate, when its site was razed in the 1950s. Just as I reached my room Mr. Bao Shixiu of the Institute of Mao Zedong Military Thought appeared. He had said he would drop by at 4:00 P.M. It was now 8:00 P.M. He offered no explanation for being late. I presumed he must have had trouble in getting through town. Mr. Bao was excited. He had been invited to come to the United States and lecture at Berkeley, Harvard, and, I believe, Stanford. He was leaving at midmonth, when I would still be in China, but we arranged to try to see each other in New York in early July. So, because of our chat, I missed supper in the Tan family restaurant. Instead I ate by myself in the Chinese dining room. There were six tables occupied. The lights were off in most of the room. I thought about the kids in the square — so earnest, refreshing, idealistic, honest, brave, the kind I would like at my side in a firefight. Scott McLeed, the State Department security chief in the McCarthy days, had first used that as a definition of character. I doubted that he would have wanted any of the youngsters by his side, but I would have settled happily for one. They were tired and worn. There had been too many alarms, too many alerts. Their adrenaline levels had to be low. They knew that if the troops didn't come this night, they would come the next or the next. They were riding a train from which there was no exit and only one stop — the last. How could they win? Not on this field. Maybe in some future time or place their legend would bring a victory. I went upstairs. I was weary and despondent. I have a great feeling now that the show-down is going to be at midnight. There is a helicopter flying over the square proclaiming a curfew, warning everyone to leave. Things are starting to heat up.

We are going to have breakfast at 7:30 and at 8:30 will go up to the Military Museum and shoot some of the artifacts there. I look forward to that and to seeing the museum's director, Qin Xinghan, my wonderful friend from the Long March. I have in my bag a souvenir of that march. It is the old pacemaker that I had implanted in 1975 and that has carried me through nearly fourteen years. I had it replaced a few weeks ago with a new miniature model, and now I have the old one, about the size of a cigarette package, all shined up and polished. I am going to have Qin autograph it, as well as Jack Service; Zhang Yuanyuan, who was our interpreter; and Charlotte and myself. Then maybe I'll give it to General Qin for his museum. He has already asked me to let him have this old 1942 Remington portable, which I carried through those seventy-four hundred miles of rough China backcountry, and I've promised he can have it when, if, and as I retire it from active duty. It will be good fun to see General Qin again and get away from this apocalyptic feeling that comes out of the square like an invisible cloud in an Orson Welles movie. The troops are still there on the edges of the hundred-acre field.

Day Four
June 4, 1989

■ Beijing Hotel, 4:30 A.M.

I am tired. I didn't sleep much last night and the night before. Last night I didn't even wait up to hear BBC on the little pocket radio that I have carried since I went off behind the lines to Hanoi at Christmas, 1966. I hit the bed and collapsed into deep sleep. At some moment I half awoke. I seem to remember very heavy gunfire. Two A.M.? Three A.M.? The moment the troops came into the square from the west, the direction away from me in the hotel on East Changan Avenue. Maybe. I half awoke and said "Oh fuck!" and turned over. It was that gooey kind of sleep that paralyzes you. About 4:00 A.M. I pulled myself awake. Deathly quiet.

Now I take a look at Changan. Continuous flow of people. Mostly going toward the square. Some coming back. Some cheers and shouts from the west side, I think. No cars. Hazy atmosphere. Unreal. I put on my cotton wrapper, open the window, and step out on the balcony, peering up and down the street. No lights in that big government building across the street. Sniff air. No smell of tear gas. None in the square late yesterday either. Wind may be east to west, carrying it away.

Eerie to see these people moving so quietly in the dark. All in white shirts, like a great flow of moths across the dark pavement. Mostly on foot but some bikers. Talking in small groups.

Changan is lighted by special cluster lights with

green shades. Only this boulevard in the city has these ceremonial lights. They cast pools of light at fifty-foot intervals. In between is dark. The motion on the street never halts.

I hear a tearing noise, metal being ripped, probably from a car. It is just to the east. I can't see what it is in the dark. Probably someone ripping metal strips off to use as spears or weapons. This is at the intersection of Changan and Wangfujing, the busiest shopping street, just below the Beijing Hotel. Used to be named Morrison Street for a famous British correspondent. But it reverted to its Chinese name, which means Street of the Well of the Princes.

No more well, no more princes, just that sound of ripping metal in the night.

Now there is the roar of a crowd to the west, toward Tiananmen. Whatever it is, there is a lot happening in the darkness. I am just jotting down these notes as I stand at the window. The light is on at the desk, but I am standing half-concealed in the heavy curtains at one side. Pick up my little radio, pull out the pointed aerial, and hold it in my hand. Reception always better by the window.

Can't find BBC so I tune in VOA. Get part of a report. Troops entered Tiananmen. Fired on crowd. Claim twenty-three killed, hundreds wounded. I didn't hear the start of the report. Don't know whether they have taken over the square. Probably have. It was armored troops. Odd sensation — listening to broadcast coming from Washington, D.C., to find out what's happening a block and a half up the street.

I think of all the times and places when I have listened in the night for what was happening. London in the blitz. That fantastic explosion of the ammunition ship in Algiers harbor that rocked the Aletti Hotel like an earthquake. Moscow when Stalin died, the tanks and troops crunching down on the central squares around the Metropole, as I looked out on the scene from the big window of the Mexican ambassador's room down the hall on the third floor. Hanoi in that cold December 1966, freezing without blankets, listening behind the heavy velvet curtains — for what? American bombers overhead — anything could happen.

Now here in Beijing. I go out on the balcony again and peer into the darkness. The impression grows that they are bungling again, bungling the end of Tiananmen just as they have bungled everything about the square since the students first turned out to mark the passing of Hu Yaobang. What a marvelous, bouncy little man he was. Almost flying out of his chair at that dinner he gave us at Zhongnanhai. Talking, talking, talking. Bragging about being a pen pal of Richard Nixon's, about their letters, Nixon's sending him books. He asked me who was the greatest American president since Roosevelt. I hesitated between Truman, Ike, and Jack Kennedy. "You're wrong," he said with a superior grin. "It was Nixon." I wouldn't be here on this balcony straining my eyes and ears up to Tiananmen if Hu hadn't been dumped by Deng Xiaoping. There wouldn't have been any nonsense about talking or not talking with the students if Hu Yaobang were alive and in office.

What *is* going on? Is it that 8341 security battalion again? Did they swarm out of Zhongnanhai as they did yesterday? Or have the big armored columns finally made it into the center?

Last night, just before going to bed, I talked on the telephone to a very good Chinese friend. She was worried about me. Told me to be very careful. She thought this was the night for the move. Well, she was right.

■ Beijing Hotel, 5:30 A.M.

A big column of armor just came up Changan Avenue, going from east to west, just under my window. Terrible roar. There has been artillery fire up toward the square, again and again. Can't see why they should use big guns.

Loud shouting. Bikes suddenly appear on the street again. Round after round of automatic fire down the street. Burst after burst of eight to ten shots. This is for real.

Another distant burst of shouting. Shots coming now from the east. I've never been in the midst of a city street battle. Nothing like this in the worst of the Civil Rights days of the 1960s, the student demonstrations. Murder, yes. But continuous barrages of live machine fire? I've never encountered it. I suppose that when the Soviet tanks went into Budapest in 1956 there was this kind of thing. I wasn't in Budapest. But I got there some months later. And the Russian artillery had blasted down buildings, smashed the facades, damaged the city a great deal. Not as bad as the World War II battle. But plenty of street-level damage.

Yes, I think the Russians crushed Budapest like the Chinese are crushing their own people. The "People's Army" against the People. And all my Chinese friends were still assuring me last night that if one drop of students' blood was shed the whole nation would boil over. Maybe it will, but I doubt it.

Some rounds of heavy machine fire. Bursts of ten to twelve shots. I can't distinguish between AK-47 fire and heavy mounted machine guns. They must fire about the same caliber of bullets. My knowledge of military technology is out of date. There is a whole new generation of hardware since my day.

Daylight is showing its first streaks in the eastern sky.

■ Beijing Hotel, 5:50 A.M.

Extraordinary column of small tanks, trucks, and armored personnel carriers just passed down Changan, east to west. Big noise of artillery fire up toward the square. It's like a movie battle. At least the movie soundtrack. The deadly tat-tat-tat-tat of the machine fire, the crash of the (light?) artillery, and louder booms. Don't know what they are. Something like those percussion bombs they were using in Warsaw in October 1957 to frighten and stun the student demonstrators. They sounded like the end of the world.

But I don't think these are percussion bombs. They are something much more deadly. I have no lights on in these rooms, and I am standing well back from the windows, usually at the side, so that I am protected from fire coming from the east as these armored columns rumble past. I was crazy to go out on the balcony in my wrapper, but there was no shooting here then.

Sometime — probably an hour ago — Junichi Takeda called. He is up in the NHK corner room watching it all. He told me to stay away from the windows: "It's very dangerous now." I told him I understood and was being careful. There is a cannonade in progress in the square. You would think they were attacking the Maginot Line. This is heavy stuff.

▪ Beijing Hotel, 5:55 A.M.

Still in progress. This heavy cannonade has been going on for fifteen minutes by my watch. Cries and shouts up toward Tiananmen. New armored column. This one smaller and moves rapidly down Changan from west to east. Sporadic shots. Many near the hotel. Getting some ricochets off the building. Splintering noises, probably bullets chipping the stucco. I'll look and see when it gets more daylight. Extraordinary battle fought in the half-light of those green-shaded, five-cluster light stanchions on Changan. The traffic light at Wangfujing and Changan has finally stopped working. So strange to see it rhythmically switch green to red to green while the battle went on.

It is awesome to see and hear these columns of armored personnel carriers and the small and medium tanks. They rev their motors to full power to increase the sound and terror.

▪ Beijing Hotel, 6:00 A.M.

Yes, we are getting fire in the hotel now. Takeda phones again. "Watch out! It's very dangerous." I thank him, say I agree. There is a big fire now at the corner, and smoke pours up and flattens out over Changan as though the whole city were burning down. Reminds me of Newark after Martin Luther King was assassinated. I

48

was running for a plane at the Newark airport. A young man and woman were running just ahead. "What's that?" she asked, pointing to the black clouds over the city. "Nothing. Just Newark burning down," her companion said. "Let's hurry." They ran on. Here in Beijing there is no place to run.

It's the carcass of the buses in the barricade — someone has torched them. The gas and oil and plastic are all going up. I can see the flames red and smoky on the pavement of Changan at the Wangfujing intersection.

■ Beijing Hotel, 6:10 A.M.

Quieter now up toward the square. I smelled a lot of cordite after that big battle (if it was a battle) or the heavy explosions that sound like shell fire. An armored column clanks up Changan. Smoke still drifts over the sky.

Sporadic shots. Many near the hotel. Who in hell is fighting whom? The only enemy I can see them firing at is the people in the street, people on bicycles, people at the corners in little clumps.

I listened to BBC at 6:00 A.M. Casualties in many parts of city. Hospitals filling up. When troops broke into Tiananmen, other troops poured out of the Forbidden City, firing as they dashed through gates. They opened the doors of the Great Hall of the People and of the historical museums and rushed out. (Rumors for days have said that the troops were stuffed inside these places, having been secretly slipped in through the intricate network of tunnels under Tiananmen and the Forbidden City. There is even a branch railroad line with an underground station in Zhongnanhai.)

People fell dead right and left as troops opened fire. Fired on citizens in many parts of city.

It has dawned an overcast day. The smoke trails over the city. BBC says it will have a more complete report at 7:00 A.M.

Just now a very big explosion. So big I could feel the reverberations in the air.

The daylight flow of bicycles up toward Tiananmen has begun. I hear the continuous wail of ambulance sirens. I am high enough, on the seventh floor, to hear many of the sounds echoing in the sky over the city.

■ Beijing Hotel, 6:40 A.M.

A shell whizzed past my window and down the street, whistling as it went. Must have been close. I haven't heard that sound since World War II. In fact, I don't believe I heard one that close in those days.

The fire in the buses that block the street at Wangfujing smolders steadily.

Occasional rumble of helicopters overhead. Mostly they fly from east to west, fairly low, observing Changan and the square. There is firing at a distance. Probably to the south.

People still patiently pedal toward the square. Not many are coming in the opposite direction, west to east. I can hear lots of chatter from the street as people gather in little knots to talk about what is happening. There are three or four knots of people visible at any one time. Not so much noise from Tiananmen.

I have a feeling that, as with everything in this terrible drama, the military has bungled as much as the politicians.

6:40 A.M.

Heard on VOA at 5:00 A.M. [U.S. Secretary of State James] Baker reminding Chinese that it is a People's Army. I am reminded of how I held forth before leaving New York about the special quality of the People's Army. How it emerged in the Revolution and was the chief force in the Revolution, a peasant army that brought revolution to the peasants. How there was a close bond between the peasants in the fields and the peasants in the army and their peasant leaders. It was not like Communist movements in other places; it came to power on the backs of a Communist military force that itself propagandized the countryside. The Chinese army never has been separate from the people. Its peasant leaders became Mao's lieutenants in the work of building the People's Republic. No other army and people have such an intimate, warm relationship.

What a crock! They came in like gangbusters, AK-47s mowing down anything in sight. What is the difference between this army and those of all the other military despots in Asia or Latin America? Give them the order and they will mow down their own children.

And they just have.

The sound of the ambulances has died away. The sirens have been going almost continuously for an hour. I will phone Charlotte after I hear BBC. The buses are still burning at the corner of Wangfujing Street.

Shouts of students. I dash up to CNN, on the fourteenth floor, to take a look. No one there. Maybe they have pulled out of hotel. Bump into a man. He says: "Have you been downstairs yet?" "No," I answer. "Very rough on the ground floor. All the wires are cut." What that means I don't know.

51

I tune in BBC. Some professor is talking about the concept of time, chaos, and the universe. Perhaps the universe is contracting and not expanding. Time may be running backward. A good thought for the day. Indeed, it seems to be running backward before my eyes. These are scenes that come right out of the Boxer Rebellion and the siege of the Legation Quarter, which, of course, was located right across the street from this hotel. I think, perhaps, the gunfire on Changan Avenue today is somewhat heavier than the foreign legations encountered in defending their colony eighty-nine years ago.

More clanking metal. It is the same sound I heard about 4:30 A.M. Must be demonstrators pulling apart buses and cars, to strengthen their barricades. Maybe someone is trying to pull the burning buses away.

■ Beijing Hotel, 7:00 A.M.

BBC reports big carnage in Tiananmen. The Twenty-seventh Army headed by son-in-law of Yang Shangkun. Claim correspondents lay on floor of Beijing Hotel to avoid fire. That is probably an exaggeration. I certainly crouched down but never thought of lying on the floor.

■ Beijing Hotel, 7:10 A.M.

Talked to Charlotte in Connecticut. She says a CBS correspondent and cameraman detained on Tiananmen Square. A Japanese correspondent is reported killed. [The report on CBS was correct — they were held about twenty hours. The report on the Japanese correspondent was not true.]

I hear a very loud, sharp, hard-hitting burst of

machine-gun fire. The buses at the corner still burn. People are streaming back up to the square.

■ Beijing Hotel, 7:15 A.M.

I go down to the lobby floor. Meet a young Chinese correspondent there. He says we met at the Thirteenth Party Congress, in 1987. I recall his face. He thinks about ninety people were killed in the square. The tanks mowed them down as they pleaded for a dialogue. I am not clear whether he saw this or was told about it. He says Fang Lizhi, the well-known dissident, and his family have taken refuge in the U.S. Embassy and that one hospital on the city outskirts is overflowing with wounded. [Actually, Fang Lizhi did not go to the embassy until the next day.]

At the bar-lounge in the center building there are half a dozen correspondents. They look in a state of shock. They aimlessly gaze out the broad windows. What happened? I ask. It was a coup by Deng and Yang Shangkun, they say. I am not certain of that. But the extraordinary force is not to be understated — the wild shooting is still going on. There is a big machine-gun burst as I write this — the second since I sat down with my notebook. The radio announcement I just heard, that "an attempt at a coup d'état has been put down by the troops," just doesn't wash.

No breakfast at the hotel today. No kitchen power, I guess. Only have coffee.

■ Beijing Hotel, 8:45 A.M.

Large concussions about ten minutes ago. Traffic now flowing smoothly on Changan — bikes only, coming from the direction of Tiananmen. In the area of the Beijing Hotel people are standing on the portico idly watching. Two minibuses have been pulled up to the entrance, blocking all but one of the big doors. Most of the workers here just stand idly looking out or talking quietly in little groups. As I watch, two waitresses run out of the Western restaurant and up to the front windows. What they see there I don't know. Soon they tag back to their nonwork stations.

I bump into a Japanese woman as I am standing at the main entrance, taking in the scene. I guess she is an interpreter. She strikes up a conversation with me. Claims Li Peng spoke on TV last night. Very nervous. Made many mistakes in his talk. Had to repeat phrases. Can this all be stage setting for ouster of Zhao Ziyang? She thought so. Foreigners continue to believe it is a coup d'état with Yang playing the key role.

Takeda thinks we will not visit the Military Museum this morning. We were supposed to go at 8:30, then changed it to 10:00. Final word will come through shortly. I doubt if we will visit anything today.

I am amazed at the people. They don't seem to be frightened by the tanks or the firing. Almost as though they couldn't conceive that the army has chosen them as its target.

■ Beijing Hotel, 8:50 A.M.

Hear a light tap-tap at the door. Open it. No one there. I look across at the end window, which I had opened, just opposite the door. It was not a tap-tap at the door but the echo of a shot, a quick burst just outside.

54

The tap-tap of bullets hitting the exterior wall. I'll have to look for plaster bits.

Downstairs I meet a Dutch woman: "I spent the night at a balcony window." So did I, I tell her. She had been trapped in the hotel by accident. Unable to get out and go home.

■ Beijing Hotel, 10:00 A.M.

Breakfast now being served in Western dining room. Orange juice, coffee, and fried eggs. Don't know how they fried the eggs without power.

People walk around with alarming stories. Young man — maybe American — claims the troops used fragmentation cluster bombs in Tiananmen. "They're outlawed by all civilized nations." I don't bother to remind him about the "lazy dog" bombs in Vietnam, but I will never forget Charlotte breaking into tears when the North Vietnamese ambassador showed them to us in Paris.

The same young man — terribly excited — tells me that the troops were now on the Beijing University campus, killing students right and left, random killings on a large scale. The troops don't know what they are doing, he said; the leaders have unleashed them. His girlfriend is with him, wearing a rumpled red dress. She is in a state of shock. All she keeps saying is that she wants to get back to Beida (Beijing University), where her friends are. She has to know whether they are alive or dead. There is no way to get to the university other than walking seven or eight miles. They wander away. I cannot believe either of them is up to the long walk through streets swept constantly by random fire.

Who can say what is really happening? As I write

55

this a new blare of ambulance sirens fills the air, and suddenly the crowd from up around Tiananmen swells to a small mob. Quickly it tapers off and then resumes its back-and-forth shuttle, now going toward the square, now retreating.

■ Beijing Hotel, 10:20 A.M.

There continue to be frequent outbursts of shouting. Just what causes these I can't say. They sound like responses to successful sallies against the troops. But that may be wrong. The fire in the bus that is skewed across the street just in front of my windows blazes up.

CCTV now says it wants to move us to an airport hotel as soon as possible so that we can catch the plane for Wuhan. Seems sensible to me, if the military continues to shoot up ordinary people walking or bicycling down the streets.

I keep getting stopped by people in the hotel who ask me what I think. I don't know what to think except that Deng has blown it, really blown it — himself, his great reputation, China present, China future. A big price for a night of bloodshed.

Three things come to mind:

1. Mao's dictum that all power comes from the barrel of a gun.
2. The old rule that if you strike at a king you strike at his heart (the students never struck at the heart of anyone).
3. Powerful men will do *anything* to hold on to their power when challenged.

56

10:40 A.M.

I learned that third lesson early — first in college, then when I worked on a local paper, and then in Russia. Don't challenge a rattlesnake unless you can chop its head off. I think Machiavelli must have pointed that out. Certainly the Chinese philosophers whom Mao studied so assiduously put it down in black and white ideographs. Deng understood it. There can be no such thing as a peaceful transition from one kind of government to another.

■ Beijing Hotel, 10:30 A.M.

I'm interrupted by a very sharp spray of continuous machine fire. The people had been running and wheeling their bicycles rapidly from Tiananmen when the burst exploded. I was looking out the window and ducked back behind the wall. When I carefully put my head a bit forward to look down on Changan, I saw two people lying on the pavement just outside. People clustered about and tried to put them on bicycle platforms. They had managed to get only one on a platform when an ambulance appeared from the east side, possibly from Wangfujing Street. It pulled up and first one victim and then the other was loaded on. There was blood on the pavement after the ambulance left. I would guess that one victim was dead or near it, the other perhaps not. So the shooting of citizens and students goes on.

■ Beijing Hotel, 10:40 A.M.

A helicopter flies up Changan Avenue rather low toward Tiananmen Square. I suspect they land there. Very convenient and a safe communications channel. The city is so torn up and twisted by the barricades it probably

57

takes a tank column to blast its way through. I go and stand on the hotel portico and a hundred yards away see a tired young man in tan slacks, dirty white shirt, a headband around his forehead with red and black Chinese characters. He walks slowly toward the hotel, then lopes up the steps.

On the top step are sitting half a dozen hotel people, a doorman and five others, probably plainclothes police. I have seen several of them hanging around. The student comes up to the row of seated men. They look at him without interest. He says something to them, perhaps asks a question. They do not respond. It is as though he is not present, as though they do not see his headband or his worn clothes, his tired face with its strange gray stains.

What is he doing here? I can't imagine. Are the demonstrators still holding their ground at Tiananmen? He is not running away and is not asking to get into the hotel, nor for food or water. Maybe he is looking for a missing comrade. He stands there a moment, dignified, serious, his face puzzling over his question, then shrugs his shoulders, turns his back on the row of men, and lopes back down the steps, slipping between the driverless cabs and vanishing into the street.

I know that I will possess the picture of his banded head in my mind eternally, the last of the students I shall ever see. He looked like an American Indian with his headband, the shock of black hair, the tawny complexion, high cheekbones. The last of the Mohicans.

■ Beijing Hotel, 11:30 A.M.

This hotel is really closed down. The shops are all closed. Only the foreign exchange and cashier are open.

I saw some people trying to open up the post office. No one had a key. They gave up and it stayed closed.

I would prefer to go out on the balcony, but I am frightened by this random shooting. So I sit inside beside an open window. I can hear the crowd and the shooting and look out when something is happening. And I have the little radio on the desk in front of me to pick up the news every hour.

I think this scattered fire is not accidental. It is meant to scare the people and keep them away from the approaches to the square. You can't see the guns or the gunners from here. But of course from the NHK room, on the sixteenth floor, where I'm due in a few minutes to film a brief report, it is all spread out before you.

■ Beijing Hotel, 11:55 A.M.

The crowd is thinner now. Just back from room 1636, doing a little clip on the situation as of June 4. I should have called it Bloody Sunday and touched that reminiscent nerve of Bloody Sunday, 1905, the precursor of the 1917 Russian Revolution, when the czar's troops opened fire on thousands of peasant petitioners. Instead I said that it brought an end to the Deng era of enlightenment just four months before the fortieth anniversary of the founding of the People's Republic. What now will become of the new China we do not know.

I heard a brisk outburst of fire just before I went up to room 1636. There is a fine, distant view of Tiananmen from there, a corner room. It is apparent that all this fire that we are getting down Changan Avenue comes from the square.

They posed me against a panorama of Tiananmen.

After my little TV bite one of the cameramen carefully arranged and focused his long-range lens on the square, thoughtfully masking it with three potted plants so that it was invisible to the distant viewer.

I could understand the dynamics of the crowd by watching it from room 1636. The people collect at a point just beyond the Beijing Hotel and not quite up to Tiananmen. Beyond that perhaps a few hundred hardy souls walk up almost another block, just short of a picket line that the troops have established. There is an interval of less than a hundred yards between the most advanced civilians and the soldiers, who have a line of AK-47-armed troops and, I believe, some machine-gun posts looking down at the crowd and Changan Avenue. In the square itself tanks are posted at intervals possibly a hundred yards west of what I would call a skirmish line. In the area between troops and civilians are several small red bulldozers that I noticed yesterday evening on the edge of Tiananmen Square. I think they probably had been earlier deployed into a kind of barricade, which the tanks pushed away. Several helicopters flew overhead as we did the sound bite for Tokyo.

The government line is ridiculous. They say that two soldiers were killed and some wounded and that some army trucks were damaged. This is a lot of BS. They say nothing about the students. NHK estimates that eighty students and hundreds of supporters and sympathizers were killed.

■ Beijing Hotel, 12:20 P.M.

I met several U.S. exchange students who had walked to our hotel from the Friendship Hotel, which is out by Beijing University. They said that when they left early this morning there was no sign of any shoot-out by the troops surrounding the university, as the excitable young man had told me earlier. They said that things were quiet at Beida when they left, at 6:00 A.M. But it had been a long walk to the Beijing Hotel. A short distance from the center of town they had run into heavy firing, and they had run up the ramp to the Beijing Hotel to try to escape it.

At first the hotel guards wouldn't let them in, but they jumped over the fence and ducked into a ground-floor window when the bullets started to spatter around them. They plunged in headfirst. The room was filled with terrified Chinese who didn't want to let them in, but they just climbed over them. Otherwise, they said, they probably would have been shot in front of the hotel.

The firing from Tiananmen Square that chased them into the hotel was undoubtedly one of the many bursts that I had recorded on these pages as they rang out again and again. Maybe the one that hit the two people under my window.

These people had heard that someone inside the Beijing lobby had been wounded. I don't believe that is true.

CCTV hasn't been able to find a cab or minibus to transport us out of the hotel. No one wants to use his vehicle for fear it will be confiscated for a barricade or get shot up or damaged. They don't want to chance a trip to the airport. I asked Miss He, my interpreter from CCTV, why we didn't use one of the CCTV cars. "We are surrounded by the army," she said. "We can't use our own vehicles."

It is a nutty situation. But fatal. As I said in the TV bite, we are at the end of the Deng era, the end of the era of innovation, creativity, and liberalization.

And the beginning of what? South Korea? I am afraid so.

There is a rumor that Deng is under intensive medical care. It seems a little too late for that.

■ Beijing Hotel, 2:00 P.M.

Gloomy lunch in the Chinese dining room. No fried noodles or any fried dishes. I settled for boiled noodles and chicken shreds and a bowl of rice. Rice was excellent. I spiced it up with a little soy sauce, which ordinarily I dislike. About six tables in the darkened room were occupied. I went to the lounge and ordered an ice cream sundae. Six yuan as usual.

An unfamiliar, rather chubby man came by and said hello. I had to ask him who he was. To my astonishment he was Jim Sterba, one of my favorite people. Jim is a correspondent for the *Wall Street Journal* in China and Hong Kong. I've known him since 1964, when he was my assistant in setting up *New York Times* coverage of the Democratic and Republican conventions. But he is twice as round as my memory of him as a slim, wiry, energy-active youngster. I hadn't seen him, obviously, for several years.

He said a young woman (I believe of Chinese origin) who is the correspondent for the *Asian Wall Street Journal* had gone to a hospital with one of the wounded college students early this morning and hasn't been seen since. He was worried about her. Said there were about ten Hong Kong Chinese correspondents missing. [All of them ultimately turned up; most had been detained on various pretexts by the army or security people.]

He thinks the party had deteriorated to the point where people just laughed at it. So they set out to show they have the guns. He is amazed at the unterrified way the Chinese face up to the armor and armored personnel carriers. He can't decide whether it is bravery or ignorance.

I asked him about Deng's role. He said there had been little or no bureaucratic evidence of Deng's presence for days. Was it a Yang Shangkun coup? He is dubious about that (as am I). He thinks that would be possible only if Deng were really out of the picture. He doesn't think they have a clue as to what they have lost and don't care so long as they can maintain party authority in Beijing. The rest of the country doesn't matter.

I brought Jim up for a look at Changan from my windows. Very little traffic while he was looking at the scene. Hardly had he gone than there was another brief outbreak of gunfire. As usual, not a clue as to why. Jim told me T. D. Allman was here doing a piece for *Vanity Fair.* I must call him. Haven't seen him since I went to a book party at his flat in Brooklyn Heights, not long after he came back from Southeast Asia. I've always thought T. D. knew more about Thailand than anyone. And Laos, too.

■ Beijing Hotel, 2:15 P.M.

I phoned my friend Israel Epstein, a Westerner who had cast his lot with the Chinese and had lived in Beijing for many years. He was warm and bland. Said nothing was happening at the Friendship Hotel. He hadn't been downtown since Friday. It will take a long time, he said, to sort it all out. I mention the disastrous effect on China's economic and financial position. No banks will lend any more money, and investors will be scarce. Not to mention the reaction in Hong Kong. I don't think he had thought about that. He asked if I was going to see my friend Yang Shangkun. I said I certainly hoped so (I must say the chances look nil at the moment).

■ Beijing Hotel, 2:40 P.M.

Big student cheer. Very strong. Must come from the Wanfujing intersection.

■ Beijing Hotel, 2:55 P.M.

Another helicopter flyover. The clouds are gradually lowering. It may rain.

■ Beijing Hotel, 3:15 P.M.

There are heavy shots right outside my window. I hear more loud cheers. People are pedaling rapidly away from Tiananmen. Then, after a pause, they begin to pedal back to the square.

The BBC report at 3:00 P.M. very bloody. Reports twenty bodies along one side of Tiananmen, three crushed by tanks. Army patting itself on back in nauseous TV, showing commander and men in spanking-new pressed uniforms drinking tea and going to hospital to pet one solider who has the inevitable bandage over his forehead. When wounded PLA men are shown in pictures, they *always* have a white gauze bandage over their forehead. That seems to be the requisite classical wound.

■ Beijing Hotel, 3:20 P.M.

Much firing. I think it is at the crossing toward Tiananmen where there are so many burned-out buses. Many bikes now appear from Tiananmen direction. Many clusters of people on south side of Changan Avenue.

■ Beijing Hotel, 3:30 P.M.

The big thunderstorm that has been building up breaks. Rain comes down in a steady fall. I keep hearing rumors that there has been a great outpouring of people west of Changan and that three hundred thousand troops are surrounded in a sea of citizens, unable to move. The people won't let them go. No one knows if this is true. Seems dubious. Fact is that East Beijing and West Beijing have been cut off from each other by the troop occupation of Tiananmen and by the troop concentrations in that area and the barricades.

We really don't know what has happened west of Tiananmen. And people on that side don't know what is happening in the eastern part of town. This became clear in my many phone calls to Nick Kristoff, the *Times* correspondent, who is located in the diplomatic quarter, to the east. NHK has some contacts in the western part of the city, but people there are immobilized by the fighting and barricades. Much heavier than anything we have seen or heard.

■ Beijing Hotel, 4:00 P.M.

A few minutes ago, CCTV director-general on telephone. There are two alternatives. Either we break off efforts to do the documentary and go back to Tokyo and/or New York, or we sit in the hotel for a couple of days and see if things clear up so we can go ahead with filming. The director seems to think that Wuhan could be as dangerous as Beijing. The outcome of a "factional" fight in Wuhan is not yet clear. Can't guarantee that if we go out into the country, conditions will be any better for filming than in Beijing — especially if the fighting spreads.

There really is no alternative. We will have to wait and see how things turn out. The trouble is they still haven't been able to get a bus to take us anywhere. So talk of moving out to Tokyo or Wuhan is just hot air. We are stuck here in the middle of things. That is a tough situation at the moment, but the real question is, if we can get to the airport and get a plane to some-where else in China, will we be able to carry out any program?

None of us wants to give up and go back. I don't think the operating staff at CCTV wants to either. Maybe we will be able to do some cameo interviews tomorrow if we are stuck here another day. Frankly, I can't believe the country is that shook up. I keep reverting to the thought that there is a lot of mirror work in all this and we are being presented with images that may not be ac-curate but that are what some faction in China wants us to believe in. It is, in effect, making a case. But CCTV may not want to go traipsing around the country. They say people are very angry with CCTV because it is car-rying the pro-government, pro-army line. And I don't really know the politics of CCTV. Certainly it is the kind of time when prudent administrators try to arrange to be on the right side.

5:00 P.M.

■ Beijing Hotel, 5:00 P.M.

BBC news wrap-up repeats the story of the twenty bodies along the street leading from Tiananmen. Adds the detail of tanks crushing people sleeping in their tents. That seems plausible to me. There were a lot of people asleep in the tents at 8:00 P.M., and some of them looked ill, weak, and emaciated. I can easily imagine them being unable or unwilling to get up and the tanks simply rolling over them.

BBC reports that one Beijing radio announcer blurted out that thousands had been killed and then was yanked off the air.

Called an old Chinese friend. He began to defend the troops, said that bad elements had infiltrated the student demonstration. The government had to act. It was a conspiracy. There had been thugs in the crowd and firing at the troops from hotels and maybe big buildings, he said.

I was appalled to hear him spewing out the government propaganda line and became very indignant. I blew my stack. I said disciplined troops did not fire indiscriminately into buildings or at ordinary people standing on street corners. I told him I had seen two innocent people killed (so I thought) right under my window and that bullets were ricocheting off the Beijing Hotel right around my room. I added that if Yang Shangkun thought that was a disciplined military operation, then he ought to go to South Korea and see how they handled things.

I really lost my head. Finally I got ahold of myself and apologized and said, "Lord, I love China and hate to see it commit this violence against itself." I said there

67

were two hundred foreign correspondents in Beijing and they were independent witnesses who were on the spot and could testify as to what really happened. We saw a different army than the one he saw — the army we saw shot down innocent people. He said he wanted to have a talk with me and I said I wanted to talk to him.

After I hung up I felt like a fool. I realized what I should have understood from the beginning, that he *had* to put forward the government line and defend it for the sake of his own neck — especially when talking to an American writer. How terrible! I am afraid I am getting very sour on this government in which men I have regarded favorably and known so long have played a cowardly and despicable role.

■ Beijing Hotel, 5:30 P.M.

Since midmorning I have heard rumors about violent battles in the western city, but the troop deployment at Tiananmen makes it almost impossible to get from the east to the west. NHK has some sources in West Beijing but has not been able to verify the rumors placing the dead at one thousand, maybe two thousand, or even higher.

Armored columns were said to have shot their way through streets jammed with civilians trying to halt them. I have become convinced that the fighting in the west was much more serious than in the east.

A bloody incident has occurred outside the Mu Xi Di apartment complex, on the western continuation of Changan, where important retired revolutionary figures and their wives live. I had interviewed many people in the complex, including China's most famous revolution-

ary female writer, Ding Ling, and a marvelous old economist and underground revolutionary named Chen
Hansheng, a University of Chicago graduate, now more
than ninety. The widow of He Long, a great Long March
commander medically murdered in the Cultural Revolution at Mao's instigation, lived there, as did Wang Guang-
mei, widow of Liu Shaoqi. It is the most exclusive
apartment complex in Beijing. A dozen people were
killed, it was said, outside the buildings, and several died
inside when troops turned their automatic weapons on
the windows.

This was the complex in which my friend with
whom I had argued over the phone lived. Had I known
of what had happened on his doorstep I would have
reined in my emotions. He had enough on his mind.

■ Beijing Hotel, 6:00 P.M.

For no apparent reason that I could see, another
brisk tattoo of automatic fire. From Tiananmen down
Changan Avenue as usual. And the thinning crowd scattered like chickens on a dusty road. Not possible to see
if anyone killed.

BBC said that in Tiananmen one hundred students
linked arms and faced the tanks. They were shot down.
Then another hundred linked arms and they were shot
down. It is too sad to write. These brave, innocent, idealistic kids. Far worse than MacArthur and the bonus
marchers.

I had asked my Chinese friend before I let my emotions get away from me if everyone in the family was OK.
He said, "I hope so." I hope so too.

■ Beijing Hotel, 6:15 P.M.

Sun comes out strongly and bloods the western sky, but Changan Avenue still seems fuzzy, as though the fog of battle will not rise.

■ Beijing Hotel, 6:35 P.M.

For a time I have heard what I think is the rumble of a tank column in the distance. Just now a helicopter flew over the hotel, flying south to north. First one in that flight pattern. The others all flew west to east. Changan now clear of people.

■ Beijing Hotel, 6:40 P.M.

I called Mr. M——, an old friend. He was very surprised. "Terrible situation." All night long his friends had been calling him, worrying about him. I was glad to hear that he was OK. He said he would come by the hotel on Monday at two o'clock and we would have a talk. I wasn't sure he could get to the Beijing. Oh, yes, he said, no trouble. We'll see.

■ Beijing Hotel, 8:05 P.M.

Just back from a candlelit supper in the American dining room with my Japanese colleagues. There were pink gladiolas in silver vases on each table. Not many tables occupied. The Bourbons before the fall of the Bastille, I said. Everyone laughed. Maybe not so funny.

Now we have new word on Wuhan. Situation there all quiet. CCTV will call at 9:00 P.M., and if we can manage to get from here to the airport, we'll take off.

■ Beijing Hotel, 8:35 P.M.

All quiet. Few people on the streets. Then — a wee burst of automatic fire.

■ Beijing Hotel, 8:40 P.M.

Artillery fire. To the southeast, so I believe. Some cries in the street. A cluster of people on the east corner of the hotel beside Wangfujing Street. A new covey of bikes heads toward Tiananmen.

■ Beijing Hotel, 8:50 P.M.

Large spatter of small-arms fire. I think it is aimed at the hotel's intersection beside Wangfujing Street. In the distance what sounds like heavy bombs. Maybe gasoline tanks going up.

■ Beijing Hotel, 8:53 P.M.

Spatter of fire.

■ Beijing Hotel, 8:54 P.M.

More.

■ Beijing Hotel, 9:05 P.M.

Big boom — a shell? I don't think so. Probably a gas tank going up in one of the bus carcasses. The skewed bus in front of the hotel is flaming again. Someone must have poured gasoline on it. A Chinese tells me he has been out on Changan at dusk and counted nearly fifty bodies from the day's firing.

Something peculiar going on in the big building across the street. Charlotte and I used to watch old men do tai chi on its asphalt roof in the early morning. I saw some men on the roof before dinner, and now there are lights in many windows. Last night and the night before it was all dark.

I've been talking to Nick or his wife these nights and during the day. We have been trading information about what is going on. There has been lots of firing around them, some while we were talking. They visited a hospital this afternoon and talked to some of the wounded students and ordinary people.

Someone called me just now — it was someone I know, but I couldn't quite place the voice. He expected me to recognize him and didn't identify himself, for security reasons, I'm sure. I've thought of all the persons I've phoned and it doesn't seem to fit. Someone familiar with me. He was surprised I was still here, thought I would be gone by now. I said that I had planned to go and might leave on Monday. He will call again tomorrow and see. He warned me to be careful, then made a remark about living out near the Temple of Heaven and lots of shooting out that way. That is in the southeastern quarter of the city. This was the first report I had heard about the Temple of Heaven region. Wish I could place who it was that called.

■ Beijing Hotel, 9:30 P.M.

Very distant gunfire and the wail of ambulances. Changan Avenue now deserted. I suppose that was what the whiff of grapeshot again and again was designed to produce — emptiness. The bus in the street below me burns on desolately. There was no evening news on TV. Or I missed it. Probably a different schedule on Sunday.

Town seems dead.

Talked to *Times* bureau again. They had heard a rumor that all guests in the Beijing had been searched by security personnel for photos. Nonsense, I said. There is no army presence in the hotel (yet). [In fact, the military took over the hotel for its staff and headquarters a few days later, or so I was told.]

■ Beijing Hotel, 9:50 P.M.

Looked out the window, craning to get a better view up the street. Heard a small crash. Ducked back in quickly. Heard an auto horn. Changan Avenue empty — absolutely empty.

Rumor: Students tried to escape the army when it entered the square by rushing into the underground passageway. Army put machine gun at head of steps and mowed them down. That sounds flimsy. The passageway goes down a flight of steps and then makes a sharp right-hand turn, where it divides — one corridor goes straight up and another goes ahead maybe a hundred feet, then provides another flight up to the surface. So technically it would have been difficult to mow everyone down unless you could shoot around a corner.

Rumor: Troops first went to campus of Xinghua University and then moved on to Beijing University. Both located in northwest suburbs, very close to Western Hills, which is big military complex. I'll bet that's where government has been huddled since long before the orders for the bust.

I've undressed and I'm going to sleep. No word from CCTV whether we can get away in the morning.

73

■ Beijing Hotel, 9:51 P.M.

Distant blast. Maybe another gas tank going up.

■ Beijing Hotel, 11:00 P.M.

Small armored column comes out of Tiananmen. There was one medium tank and six personnel carriers. A lot of shooting as they came up to the street crossing just before you get to the hotel from Tiananmen. They crunched ahead over the debris, passing on to the east and continuing about three blocks, probably up to the Post and Telegraph Building. Then there was a wild outburst of gunfire. Finally the gunfire dwindled away.

■ Beijing Hotel, 11:20 P.M.

That column (I think) came back. Looked like the same one. It headed back for Tiananmen and was followed by two big armored units, all personnel carriers. Maybe there was a small tank or two that I missed. There was the usual bit of shooting at the intersection. Then they passed into the square.

■ Beijing Hotel, 11:30 P.M.

Now I am really going to bed.

Day Five
June 5, 1989

■ Beijing Hotel, 3:10 A.M.

Terrific outburst of cannonading. Just now, as I shake myself awake, there is a lot of random shooting. Single shots from some kind of heavy gun and a whole column of small tanks or troop carriers roaring and revving in the nearest traffic lane alongside the hotel. I am getting very cautious. I watch the column go by through the iron columns on the balcony. Finally they pass by, huffing and puffing and spitting an occasional shot up toward Tiananmen Square, of all things.

■ Beijing Hotel, 3:30 A.M.

Another small armored task force passed by the hotel going to the square. Noisy and occasional burst of fire. I counted thirteen or fourteen small troop carriers. Dead quiet after they passed. Phoned Nick. He is trying to write a Q-head, a commentary on the events. He told me the brother-in-law of the *Times* chauffeur was killed last night. An army bullet.

■ Beijing Hotel, 4:20 A.M.

A larger armored column of fourteen vehicles came in from the east. As usual it fired a few rattles of shots into the intersection. I guess intersections have been declared free-fire zones. I could see in silhouette two light self-propelled guns. These are probably what have been making the loud smacks. The bursts land two or three minutes before the column passes.

■ Beijing Hotel, 4:35 A.M.

Can hear an armored column or columns in the far distance to the southwest. I have learned their characteristic sound: It is a *phuffle,* not a clatter. The motors roar and roar upward as they rev them. Just before that column returned to Tiananmen there was a spit of fire from the square.

■ Beijing Hotel, 4:53 A.M.

Random firing in the square. What in God's name are they doing there? The fire has been intermittent but continuous up there for more than twenty-four hours. That is not military action in my understanding of it. Are they carrying out some private executions?

■ Beijing Hotel, 5:00 A.M.

I have heard five or six bursts or individual shots. The first gray light is in the skies.

■ Beijing Hotel, 5:10 A.M.

Almost forgot. Hysterical Chinese in lobby yesterday. Probably from Hong Kong. He reminded me that last year in the hotel I had my snapshot taken with him; I remember him insisting. Now he was terribly upset. "Will you write about Tiananmen?" I said I would. "Be careful," he said. "They know who you are. They will kill you."

I said I would be careful. He looked away vaguely.

"I wanted that snapshot for my son," he said. "Unfortunately it was very fuzzy."

Three or four heavy bursts. They were very close — God knows why.

■ Beijing Hotel, 5:35 A.M.

A new kind of column down below. Five or six buses escorted by small tracked vehicles and some other military emerge from Tiananmen. They move east on Changan. Halt about two blocks to the east of the hotel. Then four sharp bursts of heavy fire. The sky is lightening but it is still very gray. Nothing on the street. I don't see how I'll get more sleep.

■ Beijing Hotel, 5:40 A.M.

Scattered fire.

■ Beijing Airport, 10:00 A.M.

I was just waiting for the 7:00 A.M. BBC to come on when Takeda telephoned. CCTV was picking us up in an hour to go to the airport to catch the plane for Wuhan. I hadn't bothered to pack up my junk. I had figured we were stuck in Beijing for another day. I listened to BBC. The death toll now believed to be in the thousands. I was astonished. All the calculations I had heard had put it in the hundreds, maybe three hundred altogether. They said that more clashes were going on in the city. I could hardly believe that, but there had to be some explanation, I suppose, for the absolutely overwhelming amount of firing that I have recorded and the astonishing concentration of armored troops. Someone is firing at someone or something. Why and what are beyond me. But I am damn certain a lot of it is deliberate terror shooting. They want to paralyze the people with fear, and I suspect they are beginning to achieve their purpose.

I called Charlotte. This direct-dial telephone system is a miracle. I just punch the call into the touch-tone phone and in ten seconds it is ringing in Taconic, Connecticut. I understand the Chinese Defense Ministry insisted on installing this system, one of the most advanced in the world. They bought it from the French telephone company. It is in operation all over China. I can bring any city I want on-line just as fast as Taconic. No interference in this system so far. Maybe it can't be cut off without cutting off military use of it.

Charlotte was watching CBS. The two CBS newsmen had been released nineteen hours after they were picked up in Tiananmen Square. Also she had seen incredible footage of the PLA mowing down the kids on Tiananmen. There were rumors, she said, that internal air service had been suspended [this was widespread but not true], that there were battles in Shanghai, and that the railroad had been blocked for several hours but was now clear. I told her the good news — that we were getting out of Beijing — and that I would phone her from Wuhan.

Then I packed up my gear and before 8:00 A.M. I was downstairs, where the minibus was waiting at the front door of the hotel. We all packed in — the five-man crew, Takeda, and myself, and we gave a lift to two Taiwan ladies who had been stranded at the hotel. They had come on a tour but had decided to break off and go back to Taipei. We were minus Miss He, who was trapped in her building. A nest of tanks occupied the courtyard, and

78

it was too dangerous to go out. The soldiers were shooting at anyone moving on the street. Besides, she had no way of getting to the airport and our driver didn't believe he could get through the streets to pick her up.

The driver was a very experienced man who knew Beijing almost by heart. No traffic was moving on Changan Avenue, and there were military patrols and blockades on all the principal streets and intersections. Many of the bus barricades were still in place. He would have to pick his way carefully through the network of old *hutang*s, the classic narrow Beijing alleyways, and try to find a path around the many obstacles. It might take several hours and he was not sure he would be able to do it. But it was worth a try. Our plane wasn't due to leave until 1:30 P.M., and knowing the dilatory nature of CAAC, China's civil air service, no one thought it would be taking off before midafternoon.

There were a handful of bikers on Changan as we started out, but we avoided them by doubling back to the narrow entrance on Wangfujing, which flanks the east end of the hotel. This is Beijing's main shopping street, always crowded with people, and I was surprised to see that as soon as we slipped into it and got away from the intersection with Changan, which was still a tangled mass of burned metal and rubble — the carcasses of a number of buses and cars — Wangfujing Street was lively and filled with people on foot and on bicycles. But no vehicles. Beijingers had already managed to find ways through their city's old streets and were out about their business despite the blockades, the tanks, and the intermittent continued gunfire.

We had made our way down Wangfujing only a

couple of blocks when the intersection was blocked by a barricade we could not get around. The driver ducked into a hutang and proceeded slowly. The alley was just a bit wider than the body of the car. The scene seemed entirely normal. Women had already hung out their washing on strings from the windows. Men in trousers and white cotton undershirts were eating a breakfast of rice, picking it out of their bowls with chopsticks. Many little shops with open fronts, shoe repair men, sidewalk quick-food shops with charcoal braziers blazing, little vegetable stalls (not much but cabbage on the wooden counter), a barber serving perhaps his first customer of the day, putting lather on his face.

We had come within a hundred feet of a main street when the driver saw that the street was blocked, so he dived back into a branching hutang and began on a very circuitous course that I thought must be taking us farther and farther from any street toward the northwest — and probably that was true, although I quickly lost all sense of direction. One hutang looked like another, lined with narrow one-story buildings, most of them old courtyard houses in typical Beijing gray bricks and gray fluted roofs of slate. At one point I noticed seven- and eight-year-old schoolchildren, all dressed up in bright frocks with white aprons and red ribbons in their hair.

A bit farther we came to their school. It had a narrow play yard along the hutang, and there on the cinder surface were some ten- or twelve-year olds playing basketball. We eased past the schoolyard and took a couple more turns, and then we were stuck. The hutang was just wide enough for us to pass and there was a dull green car, a Japanese make of some kind, blocking the hutang, not dead center but close enough so that we could not move. The car's driver was sitting in it. It was stuck. Either the motor had died or it was out of gas. I didn't think even our skillful driver could back the minibus all the way back to the last turnoff. But fortunately we had a bus full of young and energetic photographers. They leapt out, got a couple of Chinese to help them, and shoved and pushed and half lifted the car over to the side so that our bus could scrape by.

All through the hutangs we encountered little groups of people with serious faces, obviously discussing the events of the last forty-eight hours. I watched one woman with a wet cloth, carefully cleaning a wash line before hanging out her wash. Just beyond was a vegetable stand that seemed to have a normal stock of leeks and onions and celery and cabbage. Some food supplies obviously were getting into the city despite the blockage of so many roads. The hutangs were much more crowded than usual because everyone was avoiding the main streets. We came up on a string of little children with red kerchiefs heading for their schoolyard. Women were sweeping the dust from their courtyards.

At one point we came out on the little lane of the antiquities stores and restored old restaurants just north of the Qian Men Hotel, where Charlotte and I stayed on our first visit to Beijing, in 1972. The antiquities shops, as might be expected, were closed, their shutters down. I have no notion how we arrived there. We plunged into another hutang, and I was quickly totally lost once again.

Just after that we passed the body of a man or

81

woman lying at the side of the street. There were seven or eight people clustered around it. I suppose he or she must have been shot only shortly before we passed by. No way of telling why or how or who. No troops visible in the vicinity. Most likely just the victim of one of the ten thousand random shots fired off by the "martial law troops," as the radio has begun to call them.

We kept coming up behind barricades of buses, some of them still burning. These must have been set afire within the last hour or so. Some were smoldering as though they had been burning all night. There was lots of smoke. Many barricades were all burned out. Fired yesterday, no doubt. Occasionally we were able to edge around a barricade. Usually, however, we had to back off, take a turn into another hutang, and try again. Slow progress.

I keep wondering why the PLA has made no effort to clean up these barricades. Why haven't they put wreckers on the streets to haul them away? None of the picture-postcard TV shots of the PLA show them with dirty hands. It is as if they *want* the barricades in place, as if they *want* to tie up the city. They don't seem to have any patrols out to check people on the streets, to control traffic through or around the barricades. All of that was being done by the students before the crackdown. Or by the traffic police, who even stayed at their posts all around Tiananmen until the end. Just weird.

Once we got out of the central part of the city, thanks to the beehive of the hutangs, we were more or less in the clear. We got onto the main highways leading toward the airport. For the most part, they were clear of obstruction except, mysteriously, an elephant chain of brand-new, unburned, unharmed buses. They were strung across an intersection in such a way as to block, or half block, traffic in four directions. It seemed to me that this elephant chain had to have been put in place sometime in early morning or it would have shown signs of damage. It just sat there, and the crush of bicycles, pedestrians, and our minibus managed to edge around it and go on.

But who was in charge? No one that I could see. If the army had taken over the city it had done it in the most slovenly manner imaginable — as though it had some hidden agenda all its own.

I could not help remember, as we skirted one barricade after another, the manner in which Lavrenti Beria's security troops took over Moscow on the morning of March 6, 1953, after Stalin had died.

The troops rolled down the main streets — Gorky Street, in the center of the city, for example — and methodically cordoned off Red Square, sending a picket line of troops into the square that simply walked slowly forward, pushing the people congregated there out of the square. They then put pickets up at the entrances to the square, north and south. Meantime, Gorky Street and other streets were choked with troops in olive-drab, old-fashioned trucks (the Chinese have lots of them — they call them Liberation-model), and as they marched through they took their trucks and upended them across the main intersections leading to the city center, placing tanks alongside to reinforce them. The trucks were lifted one on one in a kind of piggyback fashion, very effective.

Impossible for vehicles (or even tanks) to get through. I had to squiggle underneath the chassis or clamber over them when I went out to explore the city.

They did the same thing at the radial highways around Moscow, cutting them off in two concentric rings with special clusters of troops and tanks at the railroad stations. The movement was accomplished very efficiently, in a matter of hours, without gunfire, just silent, efficient troops who had specific orders and knew exactly how to carry them out. Once the troops and blocks were in place, Beria controlled the city. It was done so swiftly and precisely that not even the military attachés in the embassies knew what had happened. Nor did I until I deliberately violated all the rules and simply went out on foot and made my way with no trouble and hardly a challenge through the barrier rings and discovered the truth.

Any comparison between Beria's operation and that of General Yang Shangkun or, if it was the Twenty-seventh Army, of his son-in-law is like comparing a precision watchmaker to a Saturday night stumblebum. Beria knew what he was doing. He wanted to control Moscow and do it swiftly. He achieved his purpose. What did Yang Shangkun and his cronies want to do? Control Beijing or simply terrify the people and kill enough so that there would be no resistance from the survivors? As a military operation it was a bummer. As psychological warfare — maybe a winner.

■ Beijing Airport, 11:15 A.M.

We are in for a long wait at the airport. Even under normal circumstances CAAC is never on time. With a war or revolution going on, we will be lucky to get out of

84

here for Wuhan today. No one, naturally, knows anything about the Wuhan flight or whether there will be one. It is not even posted on the departure list! We saw something interesting on the way here, once we had gotten out of the hutangs. On the arrow-straight road with its heavy plantings of trees, shrubbery, and flowers, I saw what I had looked for four days ago, when we arrived: convoys of PLA men. We came upon three separate PLA outfits, none of them very large, parked at the side of the road — two right alongside, one back under the trees of the access lanes. The one on the access lane was the largest — we could not see it well because of the shrubbery — but we made out a line of possibly forty or fifty trucks with the troops waiting there. No people around them.

But the two units along the highway were of a different character. They were smaller, possibly twenty-five or thirty trucks each. The soldiers looked tired and distracted, and the columns were surrounded by a hubbub of Beijingers haranguing them, arguing with them, begging them to go back and not to shoot their fellow Chinese. I guessed from the lackadaisical appearance of the troops — grubby, with none of the spit-and-polish of the TV soldiers — that they had come a long way, didn't know why they were there, and wished they could be back home. I didn't see any officers with one of these parked units. Maybe they were asleep in a bus or troop carrier. But the officers, ten or twelve of them in the second troop unit, were clustered together, smoking and talking languidly, in the center of the column. They paid no attention to the arguments between their men and the citizens, nor did the citizens pay any attention to the officers.

We didn't encounter any signs of a coup at the airport itself. There had been only the normal white-jacketed traffic police in their little glass booths along the way. Things were in a bit of disarray, but that was because they are building a new terminal, or departure lounge, for domestic traffic that won't open for another two years. Until then, everyone on an outgoing flight has to stand in line at a dirty shed to check their baggage. Typical CAAC insolent disregard of the needs or convenience of its customers.

∎ Beijing Airport, 12:30 P.M.

I have been talking with a young Chinese who told me some of the things he saw on the night of June 3–4. He swears he saw these things with his own eyes. He was standing in his neighborhood with a group of people who were ordinary residents of the courtyard. They were squatting on their heels, as the Chinese like to do, talking and smoking cigarettes. One of those armored columns — could have been one that I saw from the Beijing Hotel window — came roaring down the street. Some of the people tried to yell at the troops not to go to Tiananmen, not to shoot their own people. There is no chance the soldiers could have heard the shouts over the revving of their own vehicles.

In any event, the column opened fire on the people without halting and continued to race for the center of the city. There were twenty dead and dying after that short burst of machine fire. They got ambulances to the scene almost immediately. But the ambulances refused to take the dead — no room left in hospitals for them. The young man was in a state of shock. I tried to think of something to say, some kind of bone of hope for him to gnaw on. Couldn't think of any except: time. In time it would pass. But will something better come? I told him that Deng was in his last years. He could not go on much longer, and then things would be better. I don't really feel at all confident that they will be better.

■ Beijing Airport, 3:15 P.M.

Still waiting for the plane from Wuhan. They say it hasn't left Wuhan yet. That makes it dicey. It is, I suppose, a couple of hours from Wuhan to Beijing. Figure a half-hour turnaround. That brings us up to 6:00 P.M. I doubt if CAAC would authorize so late a departure. Hope I'm wrong.

I've been thinking about that period in the Beijing Hotel. I was not at all afraid at the first outbreak of the military terror, early in the morning of June 4. Initially, I did not really believe they were firing live ammunition. Then I began to hear ricochets from the building and I knew it was for real. But I was not afraid. Very foolish.

By the time I got to the airport this morning my nerves had been conditioned to the sound of the bullets and the shells and the roar of the tanks. I find myself responding to the sounds of the airport as though I am still in the heart of the battle. Every metallic rasp, every plane motor revving up and I start to crouch like a Pavlovian dog. I wonder how long these responses will endure?

I simply can't bear the posed TV clips of the officers in their newly starched uniforms, not a speck of dust, not a stain of grease, not a drop of blood (but poorly fitting uniforms; just pulled off the warehouse shelf), visiting wounded PLA men with their stagey bandages. Of course, I'm sorry for the PLA guys. "Just carrying out orders."

Some orders! If you asked one about the Nuremberg convention (which permits military men to refuse to obey unlawful orders) they would look at you with glazed eyes. They have never heard of Nuremberg or the convention. And if one had refused an order he would have been shot quicker than a Beijing student. The sight of the officers presenting their men with bouquets of flowers and pretty nurses in white uniforms and caps simpering at their sides — revolting!

And the next frame shows bodies on the street like bags of rags, or carbonized soldiers sitting at the wheels of their carbonized trucks, stiff, erect, and black. Most ghoulish: a soldier boy, naked, guts ripped out, penis bulging upright.

On the next channel a British TV serial is playing, with Chinese dubbing. A World War I scene, smart putteed Brits with swagger sticks visiting a hospital in beautiful rural England populated by sexy, flirty nurses. Take your choice: Channel 3 or Channel 4. Or a solid U.S. soap opera, lots of kitchen scenes of family arguments, all Chinese-dubbed. Or on Channel 1, flashy swordplay from a costume drama of the Three Kingdoms. I punched those buttons last night in room 735 while columns of armor rumbled down Changan Avenue and machine fire burst out again and again.

■ Wuchang, Center of the World Guesthouse,
   9:30 P.M.

Here we are in this curiously named guesthouse,
Hua Juang, "the Center of the World." Seldom have I
felt farther from the center of the world than this evening.
We landed here at 8:00 P.M. after an uneventful flight
from Beijing. The only surprises were that we flew at all
and that we did not break the landing gear when we
touched down so hard. Ten MiG fighters lined up in front
of the terminal. One took off as we waited for our
luggage.

There had been constant rumors during the day that
domestic flights were suspended. A good many flights
were canceled, but what else is new for CAAC. It is
agreed by Chinese and foreigners alike that it is the
worst-managed airline in the world. There were many
empty seats on the Wuhan plane. Ordinarily CAAC *never*
lets a plane fly that is not jammed.

Whatever is going on in Wuchang, I can't figure it
out. The official who met us started talking about the
"dangerous" situation in Hankou, across the Yangtze,
too dangerous for us to go there. Wuhan is a twin city:
Wuchang lies on one side of the river, Hankou on the
other. They are connected by a famous bridge. Things
were so dangerous in Hankou, the official insisted, that
they had been compelled to cancel the big banquet that
had been planned for tonight, as well as our rooms at the
city's fine joint-venture hotel. Instead we were being put
up at this guesthouse, which belongs to the Administration Bureau for Electricity, that is, the local Con Ed.

I did not believe conditions were so bad, but after many questions our host finally revealed that traffic across the Wuhan bridge, centerpiece of the regime's first five-year plan (built from Soviet plans with the aid of Soviet engineers and steel girders), was under the authority of students who had seized the crossing. He would say no more. Well, I said, let's change the subject — how about conditions in Beijing? "I'm not even going to talk about the situation in Beijing," the poor man wailed. He was in a funk, and there was no sense in prodding him. I hoped he would make a bit more sense in the morning.

Meantime he led us — or tried to lead us — to the Center of the World Guesthouse. Being from Hankou, he had some difficulty in finding the Center of the World. Finally we arrived, and it proved to be an entirely satisfactory provincial hotel. No frills, but clean and comfortable and on-line with the wondrous direct-dial telephone system.

I pulled out my trusty 1942 Remington portable and batted out an op-ed piece for the *New York Times* in which I proclaimed the end of the Deng Xiaoping era of enlightenment and the opening of a new regime that would be run by the doctrine of "authoritarianism" (which sounded suspiciously like that of Chiang Kaishek) and on the "South Korean model" — both of which had been receiving a great deal of public attention and evaluation in recent months.

I called Charlotte to tell her I had made it safely out of Beijing and then dictated my piece to New York as smoothly as if I had been in Connecticut. If I had had a portable computer I could have sent it that way. Extraordinary.

90

Day Six
June 6, 1989

■ Wuchang, 8:00 A.M.

Anniversary of D day, 1944. I was in Poltava, in the Ukraine, that day. Tremendously excited by the first flight of U.S. bombers to land at the new shuttle bases. Then we heard about D day and persuaded the Russians to take us back to Moscow, where people had exploded in excitement. Forty-five years ago. Another world, another war.

I still can't get the situation of the Wuhan bridge straight. Our man claims thousands of students are on the bridge blocking traffic. But he also says they let workers and students and ordinary people pass across, not soldiers. Someone broke the rear window of the officials' minibus when they came over. Not clear why. The Wuhan bridge is a double one — vehicular and pedestrian traffic on the top level, train traffic on the one below.

I heard train whistles and train rumblings last night, so I am sure the trains are going through. Our man indignantly said, Of course the trains are running, never been interrupted. But BBC says the train traffic was twice interrupted for several hours. Also reports that Shanghai students have halted rail traffic there by lying on the rails.

Someone put the fear of God into our little host, who is a Hubei provincial official. He said that normally they would not have received us, but since the Japanese and Mr. Salisbury are known as friends of China they "let us come." The official talked a lot more freely today than last night. He said the students took control of the bridge three or four days ago when they heard of the "Beijing events." Probably they seized it on Sunday afternoon. Thousands line the bridge in the daytime, but they dwindle away at night.

So far as I can find out there has been no attempt by the military to use force to open the bridge. Maybe the MiG fighter-bombers are flown over it to intimidate the students. But maybe not. I can't imagine the army using bombs or artillery that would damage this historic monument to early days of the Republic. This was the place, so it was said, that Deng chose to call together his army regional commanders for their pledges of support for his crackdown. I don't think Deng would have called the meeting here if there were any real question of security. Deng's younger brother was mayor of Wuhan for several years and still lives here.

Later on I heard that the students thought Deng's son, Deng Pufang, was in Wuhan and that they were stopping trains and searching for him. In fact, Pufang had been in Wuchang ten days earlier, presiding over an athletic competition, but he had left before the crisis arose.

■ Wuchang, 9:30 A.M.

Everyone here has heard of the Tiananmen massacre. Apparently the students got their first word from BBC, followed by many calls from friends in Beijing.

Not really much new this morning. Worldwide indignation directed principally at the PLA. The Soviet

Union, Hungary, and Yugoslavia have joined in. Beijing seems totally isolated internationally.

The Chinese authorities seem to be waging a low-scale war against the correspondents, trying to get them out of the Beijing Hotel, which is too much front and center. Too easy to see from the Beijing Hotel windows how the government lies. But actually any correspondent in the hotel now is immobilized because the army has extended its perimeter along Changan down past Wangfujing Street, which puts the hotel behind the lines. No one can get in or out except with great difficulty and some danger from the trigger-happy soldiers.

They have put twenty tanks on an expressway overpass overlooking Beijing's diplomatic area. This is clearly to intimidate the diplomats and the correspondents in that zone. If the army were really fighting a civil war, the move would make some sense, because an enemy might approach from that direction. But since there is no enemy the move must be interpreted as directed against the foreigners. Or the tank deployment might be designed to convince the diplomats that the PLA is fighting a real enemy: There is a lot of Chinese shadow play in all this.

We have not yet arrived at the situation that led to the Legation siege, in 1900, but little cat steps are taking us in that direction.

They say lots more troops were brought into Beijing last night, firing as they came, killing and wounding more civilians. The principal butchers are said to be the Twenty-seventh Army, but I wonder about that. My theory is that all are acting on strict orders, and I don't see how one division can be distinguished from another. The order obviously is that anyone on the street is an enemy. Fire first and don't bother to ask questions.

It is a war zone and a war is going on. You don't go out in the battlefield, turn over the dying, and ask "Who are you?" You bury your dead, burn the other bodies, collect your medals, and go on to the next assignment.

Not one word up to now from Deng Xiaoping. Lots of rumors that he is dead or incapacitated. I don't believe them. Yang Shangkun has said nothing. Neither has Li Peng. I see no evidence of a military split. So far as I can see, the Gang of Three — Deng, Yang, and Li — are in charge, and everything is going the way they want it to go.

■ Wuchang, 5:00 P.M.

Toured Wuchang, and I think our Hubei friend has greatly exaggerated the situation. I think that may go for other provincial areas. Not the chaotic picture he painted. That big Wuhan bridge has stood for more than thirty years — started in 1955 in the first batch of projects Khrushchev gave Mao after Stalin died. It has been in service since 1957 and is still in service, so far as I can ascertain.

Today I saw the bridge with my own eyes, and in fact, the NHK team took several bites of me posed against it for background while I talked about a really big Wuhan crisis, in 1967, during the Cultural Revolution. The local commander in chief and the local authorities, backed by a special militia called the One Million

Heroes, stood up on their hind legs and refused to follow Beijing's directives. They kidnapped a couple of Beijing officials, almost did the same with Zhou Enlai, and ended up in a faceoff with army troops, naval units on the Yangtze, and an air force before a shaky compromise was hammered out.

That was a real rebellion. This one seems to me to have been pretty adolescent, but it succeeded in scaring the pants off the local hierarchy. It is true that there were two stoppages of several hours each in rail traffic. The rail link of the bridge is guarded by special railroad police. No evidence they did anything to prevent the stoppages, which seem to have been accomplished by lifting a rail on the approaches to the bridge. At least in a newsreel clip I saw they showed about a hundred of those well-dressed, well-pressed PLA men, hand lifting a rail and nestling it into place, thus restoring service over the bridge.

The bicycle-pedestrian level of the bridge is controlled in some manner by the students, but judging by the traffic I saw from the riverbank where we did our filming, there is a continuous flow across the bridge that includes trucks, vans, minibuses, and ordinary vehicles, as well as throngs of people.

At the terminus of the bridge in the center of the Wuchang shopping area, I saw a throng of people sturdily climbing the long flight of steps to bridge level. No impediments. Nothing in sight that I would not have expected at any time on any day. I would say no more interference with traffic than a normal rush hour on the West Side approaches to the George Washington Bridge, bearing in mind that most of the Chinese bridge crossers are pedestrians and cyclists.

I think the "seizure" of the bridge by the students is not practical but symbolic — as is so much of this revolution, if indeed it can be called that. It is hard to define what is happening here. Maybe it should be called a coup d'état against the perceived danger that a revolution might occur.

The important thing I found was in the main shopping street, where five or six clusters of people gathered around students who had put up posters about the Tiananmen massacre. Some of them were boldly headlined "NINE WUHAN STUDENTS KILLED IN TIANANMEN" and gave the names. No way of checking that death toll, but it seemed modest considering how many Wuhan students went to Beijing. The students were exhorting the crowds and telling them in realistic, even lurid language of the massacre. I don't know whether any of the speakers had been at Tiananmen. Maybe some had. There were slogans chalked up on the walls:

— Down with Li Peng!
— Good news: Deng Xiaoping's death is near!
— Against Violence by Fascists!
— White Cat, Black Cat,
    Any Cat Is a Bad Cat!

This last is a play on Deng's famous statement: It doesn't matter whether the cat is black or white so long as it catches the mouse. It had been spray-painted on the side of a bus. There were many "Down with Li Peng"s.

None of the slogans mentioned General Yang Shangkun. At many places where students were speaking, traffic was blocked, and we had to pick our way carefully.

As we drove through the city we encountered a funeral procession — big Chinese paper wreaths in front. It was dedicated to the fallen of Tiananmen. The funeral ceremony had been conducted in one of the public squares, and now the delegations of students and workers had broken up into individual units and were beginning to disperse. Each had its own banner, identifying the unit. Most but not all were students. They carried great flowing red banners.

I don't know how many had participated in the meeting — certainly a couple of thousand, maybe more. When the meeting ended the students and others began to march back to their homes or workplaces. Many stopped passing trucks, asked for rides, and piled aboard at the invitation of the drivers. Here was evidence of something that should have deeply disturbed the Beijing junta — an alliance of students and workers already seemed to be in the making in Beijing, and here, hundreds of miles away in the big steel center of Wuhan, was tangible evidence that the alliance had spread into the provinces.

There were no military around and no police. In fact, I hardly saw a traffic officer in the main streets, although traffic was flowing without any impediment. But appearances were deceptive. Our camera crew wanted to shoot some sequences at the party headquarters to be used in the cameo about the 1967 crisis. Permission was refused. It turned out the party chiefs were having an emergency meeting. I guessed that the next day there might be more of a show of security than we had seen so far.

I was amazed to see an old statue of Mao in the courtyard of party headquarters. You don't find those very often. The only one I know of in Beijing is in the courtyard of the Ministry of Forestry, an otherwise pleasant locale.

We wanted to take some panorama shots from the heights over the city, but that was refused on security grounds, although officials did let the crew climb to the top of a six-story building under construction in the center of town, where they got some excellent views. There was a good bit of fussing over where to position me for some more bites about Wuhan. Finally, a site was selected in the old foreign quarter with a rather imposing building that once housed the Shanghai & Hong Kong Bank in the background. The colonial architecture is preserved; the building itself houses some nondescript shops.

■ Wuchang, 8:50 P.M.

Huang Jinaming, our marvelously hyperkinetic liaison from CCTV who handles our local arrangements, was excited about the 7:00 P.M. news. He thought something important would be announced. We watched. It wasn't, to his (and our) regret. We thought Deng Xiaoping might make an appearance.

Later in the evening, however, Beijing TV did run a clip of a meeting of the State Council presided over by Li Peng, with Yao Yilin, an old hard-liner and economist;

President Yang Shangkun; and Tian Jiyun, another hard-liner, attending. Maybe this was what Huang Jinaming was expecting. He has a wonderful name — roughly translated it means "A bright tomorrow will be built by me." Hope it is prophetic. China will need young men like him once this crisis is over.

The news was delivered in deadpan fashion by the professional young men and young women who are the regular evening news readers. The army has taken over CCTV for all practical purposes. Army tanks jam its courtyard, army men are stuffed into every broadcast studio. No CCTV camera crews are allowed out to cover stories. Only army TV crews. No CCTV news or commentary is permitted, only copy provided by the army. One evening they even had an army announcer reading the news on radio. The army must be frightened that the world will find out what it already knows — about the PLA atrocities.

The army news consists of puff pieces and atrocity stories — that "bad men" stripped an army man of his uniform and then killed him. Maybe the army is right to suspect a lack of sympathy for their lies among the CCTV staff. A couple of weeks ago, in one of the Beijing demonstrations before the massacre, a delegation of CCTV people marched with a banner that read: "Don't believe what we write; We write lies." If that was true two weeks ago, it is a thousand times more true today. The latest army propaganda line is that there was no Tiananmen massacre. Nobody killed. Nobody!

Very peculiar conduct in Beijing. Is Deng Xiaoping dead?

Wuhan TV tonight said the railroad bridge was closed for seven hours on Sunday, June 4, and four hours today. They got the word of Tiananmen down here very fast.

Met some American students who are trying to get to Beijing. They said they couldn't get there by train so were taking the riverboat to Shanghai. A Taiwan man and his daughter told us they were unable to get from Hangzhou to Canton and thus would have to return to Taiwan via Shanghai. This would indicate rail disruption is widespread, but, I think, this is very temporary.

We got word that NHK has evacuated its suite at the Beijing Hotel. Too hard to get in and out. They will try to work from their home apartments. Not so easy. The Beijing Hotel is just about empty. The erratic shooting down Changan continues. No more sign of a reason for it now than before. I talked to Nick in Beijing. Told him I was dubious of the function of those twenty tanks perched near the diplomatic quarter. I think they are a propaganda prop. The guns are pointed both ways — toward the quarter and away from it. Nick believes they have been fired occasionally away from the quarter. For what reason? Nick says that if the Thirty-eighth Army should come to attack the Twenty-seventh it would come that way. But I don't think there is any division among the armies. The army continues to shoot passing pedestrians as if that were its function. Perhaps it is.

Here is an odd element. A correspondent who lives at the Beijing Hotel and who is fluent in Chinese happened to pass through one of the service rooms of the hotel and saw maids sewing those great red streamers

100

that the hotel hangs on the front of the building for holidays. These had the legend "Welcome PLA." A plain-clothes man warned the correspondent not to mention what he had seen. This was one week before the June 4 Tiananmen massacre. But the red streamers were never hung on the hotel — at least not up to the time we left. Now maybe they are in place.

■ Wuchang, 9:30 P.M.

Our jittery host gave us the news: We will cross the bridge at 6:30 A.M. tomorrow and have our breakfast on the Hankou side. Fact is, we have to cross the bridge because we are taking the river steamboat tomorrow morning to Jiujiang, which is downstream about a twelve- or thirteen-hour ride, and the terminal is on the Hankou side.

At dinner I began to quiz our Hubei man about Hankou. For a brief period in history "Red Hankou" was the capital of the revolutionary world. Every kind of radical could be found here. This was where Mikhail Borodin, the adviser Stalin sent to Dr. Sun Yatsen, made his last stand. This was where all of the Soviet advisers congregated after Chiang Kaishek butchered the Communists in Shanghai, in 1927. Here you could find Jimmy Sheehan; the remarkable American female Communist Rayna Prohme; her husband, Bill; Soong Chingling, so young and freshly widowed by Sun Yatsen; Anna Louise Strong; the Chens (Eugene Chen was foreign minister of the Hankou government); Trotskyites; anarchists; revolutionaries from every country in Europe and America. A brief but dazzling period in revolutionary history, in

Chinese history. I asked our man if it had left any mark on Hankou. He looked at me in baffled ignorance. He didn't know what I was talking about. Finally he said yes, he had heard that some foreign experts had come to Hankou in the early days to help develop China's agriculture and industry. I sighed. He still hadn't a clue. He was just trying to put foreigners into some context that he could understand.

The notion of an Internationale, one that was really sincere when it sang that song, that went from one country to another trying to bring a revolution to a boil, was beyond his powers of understanding. They just piss their revolutionary traditions down the memory hole and reach for another bit of boilerplate from the agitprop shelf. How sad.

Day Seven
June 7, 1989

■ Hankou, 6:30 A.M.

We got up at 5:00 A.M. and crossed the Wuhan bridge at fifty miles an hour, the bridge clean as a whistle, a few early birds pedaling their cycles to work, a few trudging along. The reason we got up so early and whizzed across in the still murky dawn was, our Hubei friend insisted, because he had heard there was going to be a student demonstration at 6:00 A.M. and also there was supposed to be a strike of some workers.

We saw no sign of either. No sign of anyone interfering with traffic. Just a lot of weary people slogging off to work. Here and there groups of two or three squatting beside the roadway talking. I lost my temper at the Hubei man when he led us to a dark and empty second-class hotel, dumped us in a "meeting room," and said he had to run back to Wuchang because the minibus belonged to Wuchang and had to be returned at the first moment. I told this character I had been in Wuhan three times. The first was during the Cultural Revolution, and my treatment now reminded me of that initial visit. Although Premier Zhou Enlai himself had instructed the Wuhan authorities to show me their city and give me interviews, no one did. I got no cooperation from anyone; didn't get a single thing I wanted done. Those were the Cultural Revolution days. Last year I had come back, and it could not have been better. I met the governor-general and we did everything we came to do. I thought Wuhan had changed. But I was wrong. He had showed me that Wuhan was right back at square one, the same rude and unpleasant place it had been during the Cultural Revolution. That didn't budge him. He gave me a stony stare, a weak handclasp, and took to his heels. What a country! I am down. Waiting in a dismal "meeting room." Breakfast is supposed to be at 9:00 A.M. I wonder. I need something to raise my energy levels.

Last night the official government spokesman on TV said twenty-three students had been killed. Most of those killed were "bandits." He said five thousand PLA men had been wounded along with three thousand Beijingers, including students and "bandits."No definition of the difference between a bandit and a student. Echoes of Chiang Kaishek: He always called the Communists bandits. Mao was the "Number One bandit." Chiang put a price on their heads, just as he did for other criminals. Gradually he began calling them red bandits. I guess we have another example of the more things change, the more they stay the same.

More rumors of Deng's death. Not true. Only brain dead. He may not even be in Beijing. Mao always got out of town before some particularly odious crime was going to be perpetrated at his orders. Ordinarily at this season Deng would be at Beidaihe, the seashore resort on the pleasant Bohai Bay coast.

There was a curious announcement the other day that, in order to economize, government departments that normally move headquarters personnel to Beidaihe for the summer would not do so. Nothing in that to keep

Deng from his favorite swimming spot, even farther than usual from prying eyes.

A government spokesman last night said China was perfectly capable of going it alone, doesn't need financial support from anyone. If foreign investors want to pull out — let them. I don't think any of the Chinese economists would buy that. Certainly not Rong Yiren, head of China's multibillion-dollar international investment trust (CITIC), who is operating all over the world with heavy investments in Hong Kong and a good many in the United States. He runs on government subventions, but those funds must be borrowed in the international market. Although CITIC generates a goodly amount of foreign exchange for China, it needs a big foreign exchange inflow to keep the cash flow going. Rong competes and cooperates with such big outfits as Shearson Lehman and the large English investment firms, not to mention the more conservative of Hong Kong's high flyers. I know that what has been happening is not at all to his taste, and he made this evident a couple of weeks ago by putting his name to a take-it-easy petition. He will have a few explanations to make. But the government will have a few to make to him if it doesn't want to kill off the goose that lays all those golden eggs.

■ Aboard Dong Fang Hong Steamboat #26 (*The East Is Red*), en route to Jiujiang, 12:00 P.M.

Hard to believe anyone on this backwater riverboat that plies the waters between Chongqing and Shanghai has heard of the Tiananmen massacre. But I'm wrong. Almost everyone, it seems, has heard, and they are upset. This boat is a duplicate of the one Charlotte and I took last year from Chongqing to Wuhan but not quite as nice. Second class is the top class. We have inside second-class staterooms. Hot. Outside ones are not bad. There are some Hong Kong Chinese aboard. Very upset. A New Zealand couple who think China marvelous whatever she does and a French filmmaker who says nothing, spending his time reading a French detective story.

The other five classes, including a great many deck passengers who sprawl on the floor in the stairwells and public passages, are Chinese. They talk quietly — about Tiananmen. I don't think they are afraid to talk to each other, because they are random passengers, together for a few hours, haven't exchanged names, will never see each other again.

If the campaign of intimidation spreads to the countryside, as I am certain it will — they will shut up. Nobody in China talks when the government holds an AK-47 to his or her head. The Cultural Revolution is only ten years past. Anyone eighteen or twenty years old has a memory of that. Probably the anti-rightist campaign of 1957 is beyond the memory of 90 percent of the deck passengers. I would say their average age is about twenty-five or twenty-six. These Chinese generations race by so rapidly. And the anti-rightist campaign — really a forerunner of the Cultural Revolution — was directed at intellectuals.

Not many intellectuals in this crowd. Mostly peasants and workers. More workers than peasants, probably, and a goodly number of unemployed, moving from city to city looking for work. Shanghai is a great magnet.

It has been shifting people out of town but it is still believed to have a couple of million unemployed.

Beijing has a million out of work, and I am sure that a lot of those the TV is now calling bandits are unemployed youth. They have nothing to do, and the excitement of brisk rock throwing or setting buses on fire would attract them.

We will never know to what extent the floating unemployed played a role in Tiananmen. But the government knows. It knew they were a critical problem, along with the high food prices, the rigid wage structure, and anger about graft and corruption at the top.

But down at this level Tiananmen sounds another note: a note of warning to the peasants. Never have they had it so good as under Deng Xiaoping. We saw it in 1984, on our Long March through the backcountry. Even in provinces like Jiangxi, Guizhou, and the mountainous reaches of Sichuan and Gansu, we saw the peasants prospering as they never have in the history of China.

I had asked Zhao Ziyang about this when I met with him just after the 1987 Thirteenth Party Congress. Had there ever been a period of greater prosperity than Deng had brought to the countryside with his profit-oriented policies? He recollected that around the year A.D. 1600, in the Ming Dynasty, there was supposed to be so much grain in the state granaries that it rotted. But certainly there had been nothing like that in the Ching Dynasty, which followed the Ming. As far as the Communist period was concerned, the years 1950–55 had been good, but Zhao seemed to agree with me that the Deng era had been the best.

What was plain in the quiet talk of the peasants was that they were disturbed by Tiananmen because it might, one way or another, bring an end to the policies that have given them new brick houses, new washing machines, color TVs, and even store-bought beds. Trouble in Beijing bothered them. It had a way of developing into trouble for them.

The dining room of this boat is a light-year away from the cozy one on the boat we took in the spring of 1988 — dirty oilcloth table, no waitresses, do-it-yourself style, some kind of slumgullion dish. No cold drinks but, thank God, decent rice. Hot, humid, dirty room.

I noticed that there was a small, rather inviting deck above our second-class accommodations. But no admittance there. It is reserved for the captain and crew. Obviously it was built as a first-class deck. Once again we have the iron–rice bowl phenomenon — a Chinese public institution being run not for its users but to provide lifetime security and comfort for its employees. We have air conditioners in our cabins, but the controls have been removed so they can't be turned on. Our energetic CCTV representative, however, gets them put back on. He also gets the crew to unlock the doors on the pleasant lounge at the front of the deck where the breeze sweeps in the windows and the chairs are comfortable. We have our dinner here. Great improvement.

■ Aboard *The East Is Red,* 7:35 P.M.

VOA reports that the Twenty-seventh Army has pulled out of Tiananmen, firing thousands of rounds of ammo as it left. Surprised they had any left to shoot off.

When the Twenty-seventh passed the diplomatic quarter it fired several rounds. Some of the shots went through the window of the U.S. Embassy security chief's apartment into a room where his kids were watching TV. Congress is set to pass a resolution asking President Bush to approve reprisals against China for the massacre. Chinese domestic TV broadcasts are rerunning footage of Li Peng's meeting of last night. Very serious runs on Bank of China and all mainland banks in Hong Kong. Bush has embargoed arms shipments to China and ordered all U.S. students and professors home.

I have been watching for signs of xenophobia, which has accompanied every Chinese political upheaval I can think of in this and the last century. The situation is delicately teetering that way. The firing on the U.S. Embassy and the compound had to be deliberate and must have been linked in some way to that ostentatious placing of tanks on the overpass.

The Chinese say that they were fired on from the direction of the embassy compound. They sealed off the area for a couple of hours searching for the "sniper" and later left with a Chinese whom they arrested. [After careful investigation the U.S. Embassy lodged a formal protest on July 2, 1989, with the Chinese Foreign Ministry, asserting that the firing on the embassy living quarters had been deliberate, that special jacketed bullets capable of penetrating bricks and masonry were used, and that the firing came from an adjacent office building as well as from the armored column.]

The real motivation for all this, I think, lies in the revelation that Fang Lizhi, the noted dissident, and his wife had applied at the embassy Monday, June 5, for asylum, saying they were in imminent danger of arrest and execution. [Oddly, I had been informed that this had happened on June 4.] The United States properly responded to that appeal. I am certain that had Fang fallen into Chinese hands he would have been shot summarily.

I do not understand all the emotions involved, but it has been clear for a year or maybe two that Fang raises Deng's hackles as no one else does. We exacerbated that tension by inviting Fang to President Bush's dinner for Deng during Bush's state visit to China last February. That was less than tactful and, even worse, was handled with a notable lack of finesse. Our conduct was equaled only by that of the Chinese, who halted the taxi in which Fang was riding to the dinner with his friend (and mine) Perry Link, the distinguished scholar of Chinese literature at UCLA. The Chinese security police prevented Fang from attending the dinner, to the embarrassment of both the United States and China.

It was obvious from the extreme lengths taken by the Chinese security agents that this was no mere episode. It was a cause célèbre. I had already heard months before that Deng had taken dead aim at Fang, that he could not abide him, wanted him arrested. Some said he wanted him shot. The reason for the intensity of Deng's feeling was never clear, but of the reality of the feeling there could be no doubt.

Now the Fang Lizhi case is front and center in the already prickly relations between America and China. I don't like that one little bit. Of course, we must give protection to this man who is so warm a friend of the United

States and a strong spokesman for human rights and ci-
vility. But it will stick in Chinese throats like a fish bone,
and we can be certain they will make a tremendous fuss
over his presence in the American embassy and try
everything they can think of to make us cough him up.

This case reinforces my determination (as if it
needed reinforcement) to get out of China at the earliest
possible moment. I may be jumping at shadows, but one
way the Chinese could try to pressure us on Fang would
be to arrest some American and try to drive a bargain.
There aren't that many Americans left in China. I am one
of the few of any national reputation. I don't want to lead
the Chinese into temptation, and I have no desire to repeat the experiences of my English colleague Anthony
Grey, the Reuters man who was confined in one room of
his Beijing house for more than a year by the Red
Guards. I am too old for games like that.

And I thought there was just a tinge of xenophobia
in the line advanced by one of my oldest Chinese friends,
who suddenly appeared in Washington, D.C., in the last
week of May. It seemed to me that his appearance was
not accidental, that he had been sent to advance the party
line. I believed this even more strongly when the troops
moved on Tiananmen on June 4. He had been saying that
the government had shown extreme forbearance on the
student question, that the students were incorrigible, that
they had been joined by underworld elements, that the
situation was unstable, that the United States had a false
idea of the nature of the student movement, that American television was to blame and had exaggerated the ide-
alism of the movement. The U.S. media, and in

particular Dan Rather, had distorted the picture and had not presented the government's side. So he said.

My friend made his case to some diplomats and administration people in Washington and to a few businessmen in New York. I did not think it would sell well, because American opinion had already solidified strongly against the Chinese government. The students had already won American hearts, and this was not likely to change.

What struck me was the attempt to shift blame and responsibility away from Chinese authorities and onto foreigners, in this case the remarkably able and skillful U.S. broadcasters.

If xenophobia entered the situation, stimulated either by the Chinese government or by the age-old prejudices of Chinese society, then there would be a very serious situation indeed. China had been through one wave of xenophobia after another since foreigners, led by the British, literally blasted their way into China for the sake of its rich trade. Xenophobia was still alive and well in the countryside, even though official China comfortingly pooh-poohed the idea.

I might have been inclined to believe that China had come a long, long way from the Taipings of the midnineteenth century or the Boxers at the turn of the century had it not been for an experience I had in Shandong Province just a year ago.

I was visiting a remote county called Dezhou up near the Yellow River with my friend the Chinese writer Deng Youmei, who introduced me to an author whose specialty was the Boxer movement. I discovered to my

112

amazement that the writer harbored many of the xenophobic views of the Boxers, believed many of the atrocity stories about Christian missionaries selling Chinese girls into brothels or slavery. It was evident that he was not the only possessor of such notions. His Boxer novels sold widely to an audience that believed the old superstitions. It seemed to me now that a government wanting to transfer blame for some impossible situation would have little difficulty in convincing a Chinese audience once again that the trouble originated in the schemes and plots of the foreign devils. If the pot of xenophobia began to boil again in China's backcountry, I wanted to be elsewhere.

■ Jiujiang, 11:00 P.M.

We pulled up to the landing here at 10:00 P.M. Seldom have I seen such a crowd of passengers, simultaneously getting off and boarding, pushing through the narrow passages with their poor lighting, shouting and yelling — the entire scene reminding me of how I've heard the old riverboats described. Everyone with a bundle or two and a box. Bundles on shoulders, bundles balanced on heads, and here and there a chic Shanghai lady in high heels.

Two short, sturdy, middle-aged women were our porters. They plunged through the crowd like bulldozers. Nothing stopped them, each carrying enormous quantities of photographic gear and luggage. It was hot and humid.

A short drive through dark streets. This is a big city by American standards, nearly a million people, but small by Chinese measure. Clean hotel, clean linen, hot water, Western bathroom. Took a shower and tried to get some news on the little radio. VOA said that before pulling out the Twenty-seventh Army "stormed the courtyard of the Beijing Hotel." Don't know what that means. There isn't any courtyard, just a parking area for cabs and bicycles and a ramp up to the entrance. Something wrong here. Doesn't fit the reports that the army itself has taken over the Beijing Hotel as housing for staff and headquarters for officers of the "martial law troops." I don't like the tone of the news. I am going to see to it that we make our way from Nanchang to Canton, and if necessary we can drive on the new superhighway through Shenzhen and into Hong Kong.

We still have no knowledge, not even any names, of who is in charge. But it is clear that a coup has taken place and that the power of the army has been enhanced enormously.

One of the Chinese-speakers in our entourage tells me that the people on the boat, the ordinary Chinese, were very concerned about what was going on. They do not believe the government communiqués, all the sweetness and light about the army. They are beginning to put their heads down and talk in whispers. They sense that the day of the informer and the purge is at hand.

The radio bulletins offer no comfort. The Chinese have canceled the visit to Washington of their foreign minister. The army has been given the right to execute on the spot anyone accused of resisting arrest.

I can't recall anything in the worst days of the Gang of Four or of Lin Biao's terror that matches this.

Day Eight
June 8, 1989

■ Jiujiang, 8:00 A.M.

Just talked to Charlotte in Taconic. She was very upset. Astonishing coincidence. She had a premonition the night before that the Chinese would hold me hostage. Then Maddi, an NHK employee, called and asked if the State Department had warned her that I might be held by the Chinese. Of course, Charlotte had no word from the department. Then, on the evening news, Dan Rather reported that the department was concerned that the Chinese might hold some American hostage in order to trade off for Fang Lizhi. I told Charlotte it was all an unfortunate coincidence. I had mentioned to NHK the hostage danger and they thought maybe Charlotte had private information from the department. The Rather business shows that I was not the only one thinking along these lines.

■ En route Jiujiang to Lushan, 10:23 A.M.

We are stalled in our minibus on the road to Lushan. Someone mixed water with the gas, or rainwater got into the gas tank. Anyway, our bus stalls and stalls, and the driver tries to get the water out by revving his motor. No dry gas at hand. Probably hasn't made its appearance yet in China. The mountain is in the fog and so am I. Takeda talked to Beijing this morning and asked them to pass word to Charlotte that I am OK. I told him I thought

115

conditions were deteriorating and that we should suspend the operation for the time being. We will (I hope) eventually get to Lushan. I said I thought it was OK to go to Nanchang, but then we should break off. I think we should not go back to Beijing but head for Canton. Frankly, what bothers me is the possibility of some unforeseeable incident that could touch off a wave of xenophobia. I don't want to get caught in that.

Start-stop start-stop. We finally make it up the hill to Lushan.

■ Lushan, 6:40 P.M.

Awaiting call to Charlotte. Must get through to her. The grisly stuff on TV, I am sure, will drive her up the wall. Our plan now is to assess the situation when we get to Nanchang. If Changsha seems disturbed — and we know there has been very serious trouble there — we will go out via Canton and Hong Kong. If Changsha looks better, we can try Changsha-Canton. Definitely not going back to Beijing.

It is quieter in Beijing now, according to both NHK and the *New York Times*. Li Peng came on TV to congratulate the troops. TV showed some of the most obscene stuff I have ever witnessed — burned bodies, carbonized, in long lines of burned-out trucks, a soldier dangling from a girder, hanged by a wire around the neck, and yet another rerun of the disemboweled young man with his penis erect. I can't figure out who burned that long column of trucks. Gunfire from another military column? Deliberate destruction by the army itself? Don't see how civilians could torch the column from end to end

116

with the drivers unable to escape. Lots of shots of "bandits" throwing rocks. Some Molotov cocktails. Diplomats and foreigners generally have cleared out of Beijing. Airport jammed. United States and Canada chartering special planes to bring people out.

■ Lushan, 8:30 P.M.

I can't think of a place in China farther away in time and tempo from Tiananmen and its aftermath than Lushan. I knew this mountain peak only as a resort Mao cherished and as the place where he brought together a big party conference at which he read Peng Dehuai, his defense minister, out of the brotherhood for forming a "military club" that conspired to oust Mao and take over the party. Peng, an honest, blunt man, had touched off Mao's ire by reporting to Mao that his much-publicized Great Leap Forward of 1957 had caused a famine in the countryside (a famine that ultimately took several million lives). Peng had gone back to his hometown in South Hunan and had visited Mao's hometown of Shaoshan and found people starving. Mao went down on the eve of the Lushan conference in June-July 1959 and claimed everything was just dandy. He had never seen better crops.

It was a shoot-out and Mao, naturally, won. That was what Lushan meant to me and that was why I had led our band of photographers here to talk about this terrible failure by Mao and its tragic consequences.

I was not prepared to find that the legacy of the missionaries lay heavy on Lushan. They and some British traders were the ones who had developed Lushan as a refuge from the boiling heat of the Yangtze Valley

(Wuhan is known as one of China's three "ovens"). The missionaries used to be carried up the footpath to Lushan on sedan chairs. They built a summer encampment that reminded me somewhat of Chautauqua, New York. There was a big old-fashioned hall for the presentation of plays, recitals, and concerts, a small chapel, and dozens of summer houses built out of a slatelike stone quarried at Lushan.

When we went to photograph the house where Mao Zedong lived, we found a large sign in the front lawn saying in English "House of Chiang Kaishek." No mention of Mao. Chiang and the beautiful Meiling Soong had shared the house and the small Methodist chapel across a little mountain brook where today I found a couple of Chinese ladies playing the organ, a new Chinese one. They played "Nearer My God to Thee," singing it in Chinese. I joined in with such English words as I remembered. An odd occupation with China in flames.

Chiang's house was the best in Lushan, and so when Mao came to power he confiscated it, living there while he maneuvered Peng onto the path that ultimately led to his death. Peng lived in a slightly smaller slate house next door, not seventy-five feet away. Later on, so I was told, a replica of Mao's Zhongnanhai palace was built farther up on the Lushan crest. We were not shown that.

Only at the assembly hall did we find mention of Mao. There the exhibit was mostly devoted to the heroic Peng. Yang Shangkun had been a leader in restoring Peng's reputation after Mao's death. He edited a book of Peng's memoirs, which was assembled from the thousands of words of "confessions" that the tough old commander was compelled to write by Mao's torturers.

■ Lushan, 11:00 P.M.

Mao was a gifted poet, and he had a strong bent for philosophy. Chinese poets and philosophers have been coming to Lushan for a thousand years or more, pondering the nature of man and the world amid its beautiful scenery and cool air. Before embarking upon his deadly campaign against Peng, his comrade in scores of firefights, Mao sat in a wicker chair at the crest of the mountain, took his calligraphy brush in hand, and wrote a bold verse:

> I have leapt over four hundred turns to reach
>   the green crest.
> Now, cold-eyed, I survey the world beyond
>   the sea.

I am going to try to argue through with myself what is happening in China.

First in importance, I think, is the role of the military. I know many of China's generals and high commanders from my work on *The Long March.* I have talked with most of the surviving warriors, some of them more than once.

I have known for a long time that they were uncomfortable with the rapid pace of change in China. Deng Xiaoping was going too far too fast. Chinese commanders, like their colleagues in most countries, are uncomfortable in the face of change. They like reliable, fixed points, not gambles.

They had to be quietly but stubbornly opposed to the sacrifices imposed on them by Deng — cuts in overall numbers of divisions, penny-pinching when it came to new technology, low military priorities. One military man had told me in 1988 that the reason for China's arms sales to Iran (which so bothered the United States) was to get foreign exchange for buying advanced technology.

In a long talk I had with Qin Jiwei, the defense minister, in 1988, he made clear that while he supported Deng's policies he would be pleased if the defense forces could have more funding. He was not willing to concede that China was falling behind, but his junior officers made no secret that they believed this was true.

I do not think this added up to an agenda for the violent coup on the Beijing streets. But I am certain the military expects a bigger role in the next government and a major voice in the choice of Deng's successor.

Mao had looked at the world "cold-eyed." A cold-eyed look at the world of his successors suggested that while they turned their backs on Mao's Cultural Revolution, they were still guided by principles that he had enumerated. It was Mao who said that all power flows from the barrel of a gun. The Twenty-seventh Army and its comrade armies, which had shot up Beijing as it had rarely been shot up, were demonstrating that Mao's principle still held. In any successor government I expected that a powerful voice would emanate from the military.

I know a good many other elders of the party, and I know that many outside of the military branch had also been restive at the changes that Deng had brought to

China. From the earliest times people criticized Deng as a "little man in a hurry." When he fell from power in 1976, after the death of Zhou Enlai, the first thing I heard was that he had been "in too much of a hurry." If he had taken it a bit easier he might have stayed at Mao's side up to the deathbed.

When Deng came to power in 1978, people began to whisper warnings. "He better not be in too much of a hurry. That is his only fault." Deng had been in a hurry. The pace of reform had contributed to inflation and anomalies in the economy, the poverty of the cities and the prosperity of the countryside. The economy was skewed. But this was true of almost any economy emerging from feudalism.

The economic problems were real and serious. But they did not impress me as being so potent as to cause China's best armored division to shoot up Beijing. It just didn't make sense.

No tie was more close than that of Deng to the military. Deng was not an intellectual. He was no great reader, unlike his fallen protégé, Hu Yaobang. Hu devoured books, every kind of book, from Proust to Kafka to Erich Segal. He read books and talked and thought about them. Not Deng.

Deng was always considered a party man. He held no military rank but, in fact, he was one of China's top commanders. He had lived in the world of the military from 1929 until well after 1949. When the military said to him, as they once did, "We consider you one of ours," they were not flattering him.

It had been the military who put him into power in 1977–78, after Mao died. The move was coordinated by old Marshal Ye Jianying, one of the craftiest of China's military politicians. I do not believe any stories of a split between Deng and the military. They worked together and played together. They were "Deng's crowd."

If Deng had begun to lose ground to some younger members of the leadership group, if the criticism of his economic policies and of graft and corruption had begun to hit home, it would be natural for him to turn to his "own," to the military, and natural for them to demonstrate their ability to consolidate his position and eliminate any opposition. That the military would then inherit more power was axiomatic.

When Deng took office he did not install a military man as a major lieutenant. Those men (many with close associations with Canton and Guangdong Province) remained in the largely unseen group of elders who really dictated policy. Deng picked as his operating officers two younger men of proven ability: the eccentric, ebullient, and extraordinarily able Hu Yaobang, who had come up through the party youth organization, to serve as party secretary; and Zhao Ziyang, a staid but able administrator, to serve as premier. Deng had had the opportunity to observe these men during 1974 and 1975, when he moved in as Mao's right-hand man in place of the ailing Zhou Enlai.

Deng made solid selections. The two men performed well and to Deng's satisfaction, although not necessarily to that of the elders. Hu, in particular, was too innovative. He encouraged all kinds of liberal thinking and took leave from even the pretense of following Marxist precepts. It was under his aegis that the party newspaper, the *People's Daily,* frankly said that Karl Marx did not have all the answers; that he had lived a century before modern technology had appeared; that he was not familiar with China and that answers and remedies should be found where they existed.

This was, in fact, merely an extension of Deng's famous remark about the color of cats not being important; what counted was that they caught mice.

There was no evidence that Hu's ideas upset Deng, but there was abundant evidence that Deng was subject to pressure and yielded to it. He fired Hu as party secretary because Hu was a convenient scapegoat for his own mistakes.

This past year, it seemed to me, Deng had followed the same line with Zhao — sacrificing him, making him appear responsible for economic ills that essentially were Deng's and based on his impetuosity, not Zhao's cautious conservatism.

How realistic was Deng? Could he analyze this, or had he begun to fall victim, as did Mao, to a benign attitude toward his own shortcomings? Was there anyone in his household who would speak up to him when he needed to be spoken to, as Nina Sergeevna Khrushcheva sometimes had spoken to her husband, Nikita, when he seemed about to whirl off into outer space?

I doubt it. A friend of the Deng family once told me that Deng did not discuss political problems with his family; there was no input there. I remembered how a young waitress in a beautiful maroon *qipao* had thoughtfully stood behind Hu Yaobang at the dinner table when Hu seemed about to launch himself over the table in enthusiasm over his latest brainstorm. She was there to clutch his coattails. That was practical; what Deng needed was a figurative safety belt.

I doubt that Deng had anyone to say no to him. Yang Shangkun had been associated with Deng for years. Did he speak frankly to him, or did he use his courtier's skills?

And, in fact, could anyone say no to Deng once he was seized by an idea? I had a friend who had lived in Zhongnanhai in the old days, the Mao days, the days before the Cultural Revolution. He said Deng was a man of courage, a man who was willing to take chances, a man of imagination. But he had one great fault — subjectivism. If he believed someone he trusted had turned against him, his anger knew no limits.

As I mused over these thoughts this afternoon, I looked out over the valley that separates the peak on which I sat from the next range, cuddled in a downy bank of white fog. I am afraid Mount Lu did not give me the answers to the Tiananmen tragedy. But it helped me sort through the basic evidence that lies behind it.

Deng had destroyed almost everything he stood for with the cordite of Tiananmen. There had to be a trigger, and, I was beginning to think, the hand that pulled the trigger might not have been that of Deng. Or the gun might not have been aimed at the target that Deng thought he was firing at.

124

Day Nine
June 9, 1989

■ Lushan, 6:00 A.M.

You pay one yuan for admission to the home of Chiang Kaishek. The stand outside sells Santa Claus T-shirts. Our hotel is the best small hotel I have seen in China. Lovely old dark paneling and fine Chinese paintings. Food exquisite. Waitresses meticulous. Bed linen is linen. Pillows are down. On TV I watched more clips of soldiers sitting in their trucks, skulls carbonized, and Li Peng congratulating the survivors. On VOA an American girl was telling about her friends. Each morning when they left Beijing University for the square, they said good-bye, not expecting to see her again. I can't get Li Peng's pictures of the carbonized soldiers out of my mind. What did they do to the students? What terrible animals we human beings are. I must get out of here.

The local interpreter tells me he has a couple of friends in New Jersey who were born in Lushan. He is arranging for them to rent a villa for a couple of months next summer.

Last night on local TV: PLA soldiers in spit-and-polish uniforms sitting on the Tiananmen pavement, polishing the stones. Trying to get the bloodstains off?

The locals want to charge NHK 2,000 yuan for the privilege of photographing here. They will need every penny of foreign exchange they can earn. The golden

flow of tourists has dried up except for the few elderly
Taiwan couples we see here.

■ Lushan, 9:00 P.M.

Very edgy tonight.

Deng Xiaoping reappeared with his elderly comrades on TV to congratulate his troops for their good job
in conducting the Tiananmen massacre. He stumbled a
good deal in his speaking, his hands trembled, and his
walk was shaky. I thought he looked twenty years older
than when I saw him in the TV meetings with Mikhail
Gorbachev just a few weeks ago.

All in Mao jackets except for Yang Shangkun!

And the oldies! No other country has ever had such
a geriatric leadership. I jotted down names and ages at a
little table as I watched: Deng, eighty-four; Yang
Shangkun, eighty-two (I swear he once gave his age as a
couple of years more); Li Xiannian, the former president,
eighty-one; Chen Yun, eighty-three; Peng Zhen, eighty-
seven; Wang Zhen, eighty-one. Not all of these were
shown. The youth brigade is Li Peng, sixty; Yao Yilin,
seventy-two or seventy-three; Wan Li, seventy-three;
and Qiao Shi, sixty-five. Of them all, only Yang
Shangkun looked at ease. Zhao Ziyang and Hu Qili, who
had disappeared along with Zhao, naturally absent.

There are some surprises — the prominence of Li
Xiannian. He was made to retire in favor of Yang
Shangkun in November 1987. Very prominent in this crisis. The last time I saw Li he asked my age. I told him I
was seventy-eight. "The same age as I am," he said. "We

are on the way out, Mr. Salisbury." But he has tottered from the brink back into the inner circle. Chen Yun was not pictured. I had seen Chen Yun at the Thirteenth Party Congress, in 1987. He sat next to Deng. Deng did not exchange a word with him, never even looked at him. After half an hour Chen Yun passed a note to Deng, then arose with the help of two nurses and shuffled off the platform, a process that took nearly five minutes, given his inch-by-inch steps. Now he is supposed to be leading the reactionary takeover.

I was delayed leaving the last session of the Thirteenth Party Congress. When I came out there was a lineup of twelve wheelchairs occupied by distinguished party members waiting to board a special elevator to take them down to their ambulances for return to their hospitals. The PLA had set up a special ward to accommodate elderly generals attending the congress.

With men whose arteries are so brittle, what can we expect? Last summer there was a drumbeat of items in the Chinese press about Deng's robust health. He was at Beidaihe, swimming an hour or two every day. He was, as he had been for years, playing bridge for hours in the afternoon and evening. He was quoted as saying that his swimming proved his body was in good shape and the bridge proved his mind was functioning well.

General Yang Shangkun was the source of several of these stories, and there were similar yarns about his good health. Someone familiar with Deng's health, however, told me last autumn that Deng had failed significantly in physical strength over the past year. He did not

127

walk well. He tired easily. He spent hardly any time at his desk, seldom as long as an hour a day. But his mind was clear.

The grim prospect, my friend suggested, was that the physical decline would begin to affect his mental processes and that he would sink into the decrepitude that marked Mao's final years, when he was bedridden, hardly able to articulate words, a pawn in the hands of his ruthless handlers: his wife, Jiang Qing, and the Gang of Four. I could not think of anything that would bode more danger than Deng's decline. Far better that he die and the succession question be resolved on a basis of live politicians rather than the living dead.

I hoped for everyone's sake this would not be the case. Deng came of long-lived stock. I met his uncle a bit more than a year ago, alive and not in bad health except for chronic back pain at the age of eighty-nine. Deng's two sisters and a brother, all in their eighties, were alive. The most recent death among his siblings was that of a brother who had been beaten to death during the Cultural Revolution.

On TV Li Peng looked as though he had swallowed nails. Wan Li seemed to have aged ten years since I saw him smiling, relaxed, cheery, last spring.

Deng's face looked dark, his eyes burning not too brightly in deep sockets, the big liver spots on his left cheek ruddy, ominous, like discolored leather. I thought Li Peng, somehow, seemed distanced from the others. This was not true, for he was sitting beside Deng. I guess I sensed something in the manner of the others, as if they were looking right past Li Peng.

128

9:00 P.M.

BBC today reported Beijing University deserted, students gone home or in hiding, waiting for the descent of the troops and the police. Security police went to the Academy of Social Sciences, which I think of as China's future. It has been Deng's think tank. Reminds me of FDR's brain trust in the 1930s. Police moved in and were said to be sorting out and carting away papers.

[Later I heard that this was not true. They did not take away any papers, but the army had moved into the academy — as it had done at the TV and radio stations, the *People's Daily,* and other papers — and just stayed there as a presence to cut off possible contact between academy members and dissidents. But there will be arrests at the academy. I'll bet on that.]

Day Ten
June 10, 1989

■ Lushan, 8:15 A.M.

Excellent breakfast. Good coffee, fresh orange juice, eggs sunnyside up, toast made with good white bread, plum jam.

We take off at noon for Nanchang in our minibus. It will be a pleasant ride through the valley.

CCTV is very upset that I am breaking off from our schedule. They say things are all quiet now. NHK in Tokyo is not very happy either. But I don't want to be around if the row over Fang Lizhi in the embassy — which VOA and BBC keep going on about — continues to escalate. I feel that I am deserting the team — which I am — but I don't want to hang around and maybe be grabbed as a bargaining chip. It would be better to be a correspondent in Beijing — out here I am strictly on my own. Perhaps my fears are farfetched, but I mentioned them to Takeda. Nanchang should be OK. The vice governor is planning a banquet.

Here is something interesting: the mayor of Shanghai, Zhu Rengji, came on TV to declare that he had not called for, nor would he call for, military intervention in Shanghai. Shanghai was perfectly capable of handling its own problems. Of course, that may just mean that he *will* call in the army. But — who knows? I met Zhu Rengji just a year ago and spent the morning talking about Shanghai's problems. He impressed me as a pragmatic,

130

gung-ho type, very much on top of the city, which is about as unmanageable as New York. I would trade him for Ed Koch any day. No fancy words. Just laid it out. Shanghai's big problem is much like New York's. The central government siphons huge sums out of the Shanghai economy and allots the funds elsewhere, leaving Shanghai without money to cope with its problems.

Had a good talk with Charlotte. She wants me back and I told her I would return from Nanchang. No use diddling.

When the camera crew was out this morning picking a site for photographing me overlooking the mountain, they found an excellent lookout spot. Beside it was a gravestone for a man named Liu Janzhang, a local party secretary. Someone had scrawled over it the words "Grave of Li Peng." Popular hatred has focused on Li Peng but I have yet to find any knowledgeable person who believes he is anything more than an instrument carrying out the decisions of his elders and the military.

I think one thing that makes me edgy is remembering the journal of Charles and Eva Price, a book for which I wrote an introduction a few months ago. The Prices were missionaries trapped in the countryside during the Boxer troubles. Every step they took was one step too late. And, step-by-step, they moved through the countryside to their inevitable fate, murder by the Heavenly Fists. Of course the situation is not parallel, but I would prefer to be one step ahead rather than one step behind. Lushan and its echoes of the missionary days probably have something to do with these reminders.

After seeing Deng on TV, I think the title of my diary about these days should be: "Farewell, Tiananmen, Good-bye, Deng Xiaoping."

■ Lushan, 9:30 A.M.

It is decided. Takeda and I will go from Nanchang to Canton, then to Hong Kong, Tokyo, and New York. The photogs will go on to Changsha. If things quiet down I'll come back in August to Beijing for interviews and the Tiananmen Gate shots.

It's a lovely day. Not too hot here on this cool mountain. Good day for the drive to Nanchang. Talked to Nick in Beijing. Quiet. Military not so trigger-happy, but a big anti-American campaign has commenced in the press. No incidents. Not many Americans left. Embassy staff cut to bone.

I am beginning to understand the feeling of the generations of Americans who have come to China and given their hearts to the country and then been driven away by some cataclysm. Bittersweet. Listened on VOA to Nien Cheng, who wrote *Life and Death in Shanghai*. So tragic. Her hopes and those of the Chinese so high. Now this horror. She lost a daughter and years of her life in the Cultural Revolution. So many passed through that hell and came out into the mellow years of Deng and thought it all behind them. How can I leave my Chinese friends behind in this cruel country? But what good to stay? Again and again I see the image of that young student from Nankai as I waved back at him in Tiananmen.

Perhaps I was wrong to talk so warmly to those youngsters. My presence may have encouraged them to stay and be mowed down. Was I just a Judas goat? The

132

idea haunts me. Did I give people hope when I should have given them caution, fear, the signs of danger? How many of those slips of paper on which I signed my name were burned by the petrol that left only ashes as evidence of brave hearts?

I am sitting in a comfortable armchair, looking out the window at Lushan, the fog swirling around the peaks, the same peaks Mao saw as he wrote his poem and, "cold-eyed," contemplated the world.

Cruelty, cruelty, cruelty. Can China break the chain? Not in my lifetime. Deng came close, but age did him in. It must have been age that robbed him of vitality, flexibility, the jumping-jack quality that always bounced him back from the floor. Something snapped. Deng fell out of sync when he fired Hu Yaobang. The reactionaries found they could compel him to oust Hu. They had Deng on the ropes. All they had to do was push hard and he would break — break, not bend. Deng was becoming a marionette, the strings manipulated by the elders and the army.

What do the Chinese people think about this? They are silent to foreigners — except for the occasional intellectual. Our chauffeur can speak for them: "We do not like disorder in Beijing."

■ On the road to Nanchang, 1:00 P.M.

We had a very early lunch, right after breakfast, since there was no good place to eat on the way. Lovely road. It's a bit later in the year than when Charlotte and I drove over this part of Jiangxi at the beginning of our Long March, in April 1984. The hills are glowing with orange-hued daisies and what I call orange-eyed susans, like our black-eyed ones but with orange centers. There are small white daisies everywhere and yellow buttercups. I wish Charlotte were here to identify the flowers.

The highway is lined with new brick houses, and they are still going up. I remember how excited I was to see new houses in 1984 — in Jiangxi, one of the poorest, most backward of provinces. We knew then that Deng's peasant-profit plan was working wonders. Still is. Everywhere I look I see the new brick houses and buildings, mostly red but many gray. Not as many roadside kilns as I remember. Probably have centralized production. The red earth reminds me of northern Alabama. Not terribly fertile.

The rice is going to be ready for harvest at the end of June or the first days of July. They get two crops a year. The first crop should be good if monsoons don't flood the fields.

We are headed for Nanchang, our old stamping ground. Deng Xiaoping was flown to Xinjian County, just outside the city, to be held under house arrest in October 1969 under Lin Biao's "Military Order Number One," supposedly because of the imminent danger of war with the Soviet Union. More likely to get him out of Beijing to the backcountry, where Lin could feel free to torture him if it suited him.

This area — and Xinjian County in particular — is poor farming country. We drive through considerable areas where the land is abandoned to light scrub and weed, the soil too poor to till.

It was not improved by Mao's wild Great Leap Forward. He turned the peasants to building backyard steel mills, had them throw their iron pots, plows, axes, anything made of iron or steel, into the smelter. For fuel they cut every tree in sight, reducing the wood to charcoal for firing the ridiculous furnaces. When the madness came to an end every mountain was bare as a bald head. There were no farming implements with which to till the soil. People starved by the millions, but they did not rise up, nor did Mao's lieutenants hurl him out of office.

The Great Leap Forward left the hills of northern Jiangxi denuded. Only now, largely by the initiative of private peasants who, for the first time in history, have surplus cash, are the hills being replanted. Eventually the green vistas may be restored and the erosion brought on by clear-cutting can be halted.

■ Nanchang, 4:00 P.M.

Arrive at this rather sleepy provincial capital. Taken to the same big old Hotel Jiangxi in which we stayed in 1984. I have a cavernous room furnished with heavy black furniture of the Chiang Kaishek epoch, broad windows, heavy dark curtains, small balcony.

What I remember about Nanchang is the fussy little prerevolutionary hotel in the heart of the shopping district, where long ago provincial ladies came to buy their silks and satins. It was taken over in 1927 by the Communist commanders — Zhou Enlai, He Long, Lin Biao, and the rest — as they filtered into town for a planned uprising and registered under false names. Zhu De, who would become famous as one of the Revolution's greatest commanders, didn't check in. He was commandant of a

Kuomintang unit, which he would lead into the insurrection. In the hotel they all stayed, very posh, very elite, until the morning of August 1, 1927, when the signal for the revolt was given. It fizzled because the local warlord on whom they had counted switched sides, sending the tattered Communist forces into ragged retreat down toward Canton. But forever after, August 1, 1927, has been celebrated as the founding day of the Chinese Red Army.

■ Nanchang, 8:20 P.M.

Just came from a strange state banquet given in my honor by Vice Governor Zhang Fengyu, a businesslike type wearing a well-cut dark Western suit. It was in a private dining room of this ugly old hotel, which must be an agglomerate of at least five ill-planned additions.

The banquet followed the usual pattern and was preceded by the ritual side-by-side conversation in which the vice governor gave me statistics on his province that neither he nor I had the slightest interest in. The whole province has only twenty joint ventures and it has no joint-venture hotel, probably the only provincial capital without one.

The strange feature of the evening came when we went in to dinner. Beside the dinner table was a big TV so we could see and hear the evening news. It boomed its way throughout our dinner, through the toasts of greeting and the toasts of friendship and the toasts of pleasure at being once again in Jiangxi Province.

It was a measure of the jitters that the vice governor was enduring that he couldn't wait to hear what was happening. He had to be immediately informed. There must be more ambiguities in the images being broadcast — political ambiguities — than I was aware of. The vice governor wanted to be able to respond to them instantly.

As it turned out, I don't think there were any sensations on the evening news. Wang Zhen was exhorting the PLA to root out "all evil" and a lot of other crap.

With half an eye on the TV the vice governor began to give me an account of what had happened in Beijing with the return to normalcy, traffic and buses flowing smoothly and the rout of the "bad men." I asked him to define a "bad man" for me. They could be, he said, some students "who had gone bad" or some criminal elements trying to turn the Tiananmen events to their personal advantage.

How, I asked, could "bad men" be distinguished from "bandits"? That was not difficult, he said. Bandits could be prisoners just released from prison, intent on committing criminal deeds. They were those who destroyed property, for example, municipal buses or the army's tanks, trucks, and armored personnel carriers. Or they might be persons who possess arms or have stolen arms from the state.

Students were the third category. Students were just naive and misled, but not, in general, disloyal.

This was presented against a TV background of more pictures of destroyed truck columns, the carbonized drivers, battle scenes, and arrests of skulking prisoners, all with guilty looks, bruises, and other marks of sudden encounters with fists or belt buckles.

I could not take this. Rather than vent my feelings, I steered the talk toward regional cooking in China, including the eating of dogs in Guangdong, something that I said upset my wife very much, since she envisaged her favorite companion, the marvelous mongrel Daisy, being served up in a stew pot. The vice governor took this seriously and observed that a friendly and intimate relationship between mistress and pet was bound to color one's views.

We then turned to the general backwardness of Jiangxi. He neither mentioned, nor did I ask about, the newest big Nanchang industry, a fine plant that turns out China's first heavy-duty helicopters for the army. As in almost every province I have visited in the past two years, Nanchang's greatest problem is inadequate power. Despite a new 400,000-kilowatt plant under construction, there will still be a deficit. All industries are on short production schedules because of lack of power.

Here was one of the real problems of China. I have found power shortages in every big city I have visited in the last two years. City after city has to put its plants on four-day weeks, or curtail daily hours of operation, or divide the weekly holiday. Industry has been permitted to outgrow power availability. Enormous amounts of power are going into the heavy-energy, low-productive air-conditioned hotels and office buildings.

If the State Council and the Politburo Standing Committee were concerned about China, they would be concentrating on a crash power program — not the murder of ordinary citizens in Beijing. Somehow, somewhere, China has got her priorities upside down.

I knew two Chinese mayors who understood this — Zhu Rengji of Shanghai and the feisty Li Ruihuan of Tianjin. I doubted the elders had even realized that this was one of China's major economic aberrations.

I don't think the vice governor knew much about our Long March. He made only a fleeting reference to it. I didn't bring up the case of the vice governor who had feted us here five years ago. That gentleman had been removed from office for a series of crimes of corruption and moral turpitude.

Our dinner included snake soup (not bad except for the bony bits of snake back), turtle soup (very good), and "stone chicken," a small quail caught on mountaintops. It was served fried in a delicious batter. When Marshal Chen Yi was fighting and starving in the mid-1930s in the Jiangxi mountains, stone chicken saved his life. We also ate hollowed-out watermelon filled with fresh diced fruit. Delicious. But every bite turned my stomach as I watched the atrocities being shown on TV.

My meeting with the vice governor had been put on local TV and promptly brought a call from Xia Guifu, who had been guide and interpreter when we went down to Jinggang Mountain in 1984. He's left the government for a joint venture operating in a dozen Chinese provinces and was now very prosperous and Westernized. They have the field pretty much to themselves in Jiangxi. He said the governor had urged him to leave state employ and get into private business.

Day Eleven
June 11, 1989

■ Nanchang, 7:30 A.M.

I still feel jittery even though the vice governor personally guaranteed my safety while in Jiangxi Province. Mr. Huang, our CCTV liaison, is very sad. But it is time to go.

I worry over everything but most of all about the kids in the square.

I got a Chinese lesson today. I am fascinated by the way the Beijing propaganda describes those involved in Tiananmen. The students make one easily identified category. Then there are the bandits, *bao tu* in Chinese, and the bad men, *huai ren*. I wanted to be sure that bao tu is what Chiang Kaishek called Mao's Reds. It is. The line between Chiang Kaishek and today's Communists seems to be a blur.

■ Nanchang, 12:00 P.M.

Heavy day of filming. We spent all morning at the Nanchang School of the Army, where Deng Xiaoping was held under house arrest during the Cultural Revolution in the old commandant's house.

I had read an article by Deng's daughter about his time here — a touching and naturally biased account — but I was eager to see the place for myself and talk to anyone who might remember Deng from those days.

The school has been spruced up since then, and to-day security (under threat of Tiananmen) was almost comically tight. We were taken through the neatly pruned, well-tended grounds of the school to a rather imposing gray brick house, two stories, a pleasant balcony across the second-floor front, gracious planting, gardenia bushes laden with white blossoms, big shade trees, cedars and arborvitae on the fine blacktop approach, handsome stone and cement wall, big gate pedestals, a tall communications aerial on the side lawn.

This was a handsome house in a handsome setting. PLA schools and command installations are always housed in campus settings, and even this remote school for middle-ranking officers was no exception, its atmosphere like that of a pleasant American college in Tennessee.

But this concern for security was unusual. Our escorting officer, Yang Baxia, vice chairman of the propaganda section of the political division of the school, was clearly on guard against this invasion by half a dozen foreign photographers and writers of his quiet, secure military bastion.

He was unable to recall when the school was organized, the number of students, its general purpose, nor which of the eleven rooms in the pleasant mansion was the bedroom of Deng Xiaoping. While we were permitted (under close watch) to walk around the outside of the house, we were not permitted to enter it. He believed that it had been remodeled and divided into classrooms. It was my guess that it was still the house of the commandant but that this fact was considered a military secret. I could see no other reason for the tall communications aerial.

Guards had been posted discreetly at each of the paths branching off from the one leading to Deng's house. With tenacious questioning some facts about Deng's residence were obtained. He had lived there for three and a half years with his wife, Zhou Lin, and his stepmother and for much of the time with his daughter Mao Mao. With enormous effort he had gotten permission for his son, Deng Pufang, crippled by the Red Guards in the Cultural Revolution, to join him. Unable to get medical attention for Pufang, Deng and his wife daily massaged and bathed their son in a vain attempt to restore his severed nerves. For a time the youngest daughter, Deng Wan, lived with them and here gave birth to a daughter, Mian Mian.

There had been no stone fence or ceremonial gateposts in Deng's day, just a plain wooden fence around the front. Within this rectangle Deng and his wife grew vegetables and raised chickens, some for their table, some for sale, because they were very short of money.

There was lots of work to do, and Deng did most of it, breaking up great lumps of coal for the kitchen stove, chopping wood, carrying water. His wife was often ill and there was no central heating.

It was a peaceful, quiet spot and probably was peaceful in Deng's day. He used one of the downstairs rooms as a study and spent his spare time reading in the considerable library he was permitted to bring from

142

Beijing. He also played solitaire by the hour. He had no partners for bridge. He slept, it was finally revealed, in the upper right-front bedroom.

Mornings Deng and his wife worked in a small tractor repair shop about a half hour's walk away. They worked until noon, returned to the house for lunch, and spent the afternoon at their own pursuits. The little tractor shop is gone now, the plant turned into a small textile mill. We visited the mill and saw the small room with a lathe and an array of steel rasps that has been kept to show what Deng did. A man who worked with him told me he was a good, conscientious craftsman and said he had learned his trade when in France.

In theory, I was told, Deng was not supposed to speak to the workmen without permission, but the young soldier who accompanied him seemed to be more of an orderly than a bodyguard, apparently protecting him rather than preventing him from escaping. His fellow workmen were highly flattered to have so distinguished a political figure in their midst. They didn't really regard him as a prisoner, and in fact didn't know why he had been consigned to these humble surroundings.

All in all, his living conditions were far better than was implied by his daughter Mao Mao's article. The worst part, of course, was not being able to get medical attention for Deng Pufang. That was typical of the cruelty of the Cultural Revolution. Break a man's back and then deprive him of medical treatment. Of course, the authorities expected he would die — wanted him to die, intended him to die. No wonder Deng Pufang has thought so much about humanitarianism and the lack of it in Chinese society and is trying to do something about the disabled. Not easy. The first task is to convince the authorities and the people that the disabled are entitled to care. The basic attitude, I am afraid, is to let them die or get rid of them as they still do in the villages — simply beat them to death or put them out to die, consider them a burden on the community.

When I visited a remote leper colony in Guangxi last summer, I found that cured lepers prefer to stay in the colony rather than go back to their villages, where they fear the superstitious peasants will club them to death, even though they are cured. Formerly the Chinese leper had two choices: die by the disease or die at the hands of his neighbors.

To me the most important thing I saw in Nanchang was the place where Deng took his daily constitutional. That had been described by Mao Mao. She had watched her father, day after day, as the sun sank, walking around and around the four sides of the fenced-in front yard, his feet wearing a path in the red, red soil, his head always bent in thought, concentrating, she knew, on what he would do for China were he ever to get another chance for high office.

For three and a half years, every day, regular as a clock, his feet fell into a pattern, his pace as steady as it had been on the Long March, testing idea after idea and plan after plan. He had spent forty years in the service of his country. There was hardly a task he had not carried out under Mao Zedong. He knew China's problems, her

144

weaknesses, her failures, and he thought he knew how to put her back on track.

As the cameramen took their pictures of the house, the doorway, the trees, the shrubs, the buildings at the rear, I stood in the yard and let my mind dissolve the landscaping, the fine wall, the brick and cement work. In their place I saw a hand-cultivated vegetable plot up against an unpainted wooden fence, a path of red earth around its perimeter, and the small figure of a man from the tiny Sichuan village of Fei Fangchu who had been knocked from his political perch time and again and never gave up. Around and around that rectangle he walked, head bowed, ready to emerge, as he did at Mao's call. He would try his hand at leading China out of a morass and into the real world of the late twentieth century, into what in 1978 would become known as Reform and Opening.

I saw that little man, that bundle of energy and ambition, who could not be held down, that pragmatist supreme, and then I closed my eyes and there appeared again the image of the youngster from Nankai, and I heard the machine weapons going on and on at Tiananmen, day and night and night and day without end, and I knew their sound would never leave my ears.

What had happened to that little man? Where lay the road from this courtyard path to the total tragedy of Tiananmen?

■ Nanchang, 9:15 P.M.

This evening the photographers have taken endless shots of me typing at this old machine, my 1942

145

Remington portable, which first accompanied me to World War II and has been my companion around the world ever since.

We wound up with one final shot. They wanted to have a picture of me standing at the window, peering past the curtains, as if watching Tiananmen from room 735 in the Beijing Hotel. The windows in the Hotel Jiangxi are much like those in the Beijing Hotel. They put a backlight on the balcony to create a more dramatic shot. I dutifully went to the window, pulled the curtains back, and gingerly looked out.

Then I pulled back and said: "If you want a realistic shot, here is what I actually did." I dropped to my haunches and squatted behind the curtains, holding them narrowly apart to give me a slit of vision, as when I was watching the armored columns shoot up Changan Avenue. That broke them up, but I don't believe they filmed the squat.

Day Twelve
June 12, 1989

■ Nanchang, 6:30 A.M.

We catch the plane for Canton at 1:30 P.M. Arrive about 5:00 P.M.

No individual arrests have been announced yet, but the TV emphasis is all on catching the "bandits" and "bad men." Hundreds are being rounded up. Families are urged to turn in their sons and daughters. Everyone is urged to help in the roundup. Professors are asked to turn in their students.

It is a propaganda blitz, and it is backed by the biggest lie they could think of — Tiananmen did not happen. No one, no one, was shot in the square. They have even put down the memory hole their original announcement of twenty-three students killed there. Now all they talk about are the brave PLA soldiers, endless visits to hospitals to succor the wounded, wreaths and honors for those said to have died. The whole order of events has been reversed. First, the "bandits" and "bad men" attacked the noble troops, who then reluctantly had to open fire. Unfortunately a few innocent people *may have* lost their lives, but it was not the fault of the PLA. It was those wretched "bandits" and "bad men" who started it.

I am so revolted I can hardly watch local TV.

And the story will be accepted by many because it is reinforced by terror: believe what the government says or you are showing sympathy for the conspirators who tried to overthrow the Communist system and the government.

Let's face it. This fabrication is not that different from Mao's claim that Liu Shaoqi and Deng Xiaoping wanted to overthrow Communism and replace Mao; or that Lin Biao wanted to overthrow the government and put himself in Mao's place; or that Jiang Qing and the Gang of Four plotted to put themselves in Mao's place and take over the government when he died.

Against the background of the melodramatic and operatic "plots," intrigues, and "revelations" of the forty years of the People's Republic, why shouldn't the government try to sell the notion that Tiananmen never happened and that these "bandits" and "bad men," possibly with the aid of Zhao Ziyang, wanted to rub out Deng and put themselves in his place?

If I have not managed to get the answer to all of the conundrums in the countryside, at least I have saturated myself in the atmosphere of China. I confess it is an atmosphere in which people find it safer simply to accept the current lie, kowtow to the current emperor, and hope that by so doing they have not taken the first fatal step toward the high executioner of whatever emperor is waiting in the wings.

One thing I think I have established beyond doubt from my conversations with people who knew Deng while he was here in Nanchang. Deng was no paranoiac as late as 1973, when he was released from house arrest and went back to Beijing at Mao's bidding. He had behaved normally up to that time, displaying no fear of further attacks from Lin Biao, who had ordered his exile. He had managed to keep his sense of reality until that point. To what extent his entire personality and that of his fellow party leaders had been affected by the atmosphere in which they lived and worked in Zhongnanhai is another question.

I am convinced that Deng was given very special treatment under house arrest. When he left to go back to Beijing, one of the old workmen told me, a cavalcade of thirty to forty cars escorted him to the airport. Someone knew that Deng Xiaoping was on the way up.

These are ticklish, dangerous times. Heard last night about a young man in Beijing. He happened to pass by a crossroads where citizens had halted and broken into a PLA arms truck. Guns were scattered over the pavement. On impulse the young man picked up a pistol, stuck it in his belt, and took it home. Two days later security agents appeared at his flat. Someone had seen him bring the pistol home. The gun was taken from him; he was arrested and will be lucky if he gets off with five years in a hard-labor camp in Qinghai.

■ Nanchang Airport, 12:00 P.M.

I bumped into a young midwestern couple, leaving China after several years of teaching. The morning after Tiananmen a Chinese girl asked one of their Chinese friends, an outspoken supporter of the democracy movement, "What's the news today?" He replied: "The news is that one point one billion hearts are dead." This young Chinese has written a declaration of what has happened, why it happened, and what he thinks will happen next.

149

His American friends are taking it out and are a little nervous about passing through customs.

When they came back to resume their teaching in December, after being away about a year, they found a striking change. They had left an atmosphere of hope and optimism. They returned to one of fear and narrowing horizons. Many old friends shunned them. Students were chary of approaching them. Something had happened. Their Chinese friends who were brave enough to talk told them that they expected something bad, that the reactionaries had won out, that the window of hope was closing.

Then came Tiananmen. Everyone in this backcountry knew what had happened. This or something like it was what they had been expecting for a year or more. Tiananmen had been worse than they expected, but it had not, they said, been as bad as the killings in Tiananmen in 1976, when the Gang of Four cleared the square of those who were mourning Zhou Enlai and protesting against Jiang Qing.

The teachers' Chinese friends hated to see them go but agreed it was time. The future was too uncertain. Worst of all was what the Chinese expected: "Once you leave and there are only Chinese eyes to see what they do, there will be no limit to what happens."

Their Chinese friends could see no rift in the clouds, no patch of blue in the sky. All dark clouds.

"And," said the Americans, "don't think that this is some spur-of-the-moment thing. They have been preparing it for a long time."

They knew someone at the Nanchang military academy. More than two years ago the officers were forbidden to listen to VOA or BBC under pain of court-martial. That long ago the ears and eyes of the military were being closed to the outside world. Since then only army propaganda had been permitted to reach the men who would carry out Tiananmen or any emergency operation like it.

■ Aboard flight to Canton, 1:45 P.M.

I've been thinking about the clampdown on the officers at Nanchang. If they were forbidden to listen to outside news, a similar ban must have been imposed throughout the PLA. Not likely to apply only to one far-off provincial school.

I have ticked it off in my mind. The calendar would place that prohibition at about the time of the dismissal of Hu Yaobang as party secretary and the launching of the campaign against "spiritual pollution" — that is, January 1987. Since the end of 1986, at least, the military has been making preparations for civil disorder and the possibility it might be ordered to take action that would not be palatable to all its officers.

Hu Yaobang had been replaced as party secretary by Zhao Ziyang, who had been premier, and Li Peng had been brought in as premier. The spiritual pollution campaign never really got off the ground. By February or March 1987 it was drifting off into never-never land.

But, I remembered, that period had coincided with mysterious on-again, off-again signals I was getting about my preparations for writing my book about the new Long March. First, enthusiastic response in autumn 1986, then a cooling off and suggestions that the project be shelved, then a gradual revival and stamp of approval placed on it by General Yang Shangkun in April 1987.

As an old Kremlinologist, accustomed to reading the tea leaves, it seemed to me that after achieving the ouster of Hu Yaobang, the reactionaries put in train a full-scale drive to turn the clock back. Something halted them — possibly Zhao Ziyang, more likely Deng Xiaoping, who perceived that the spiritual pollution campaign would torpedo Reform and Opening as well. So they went underground and continued to work for a sea change.

My American friends in China felt our response to Tiananmen had been too weak to have an impact in Beijing. I shared that feeling. I did not believe anything we did would halt the Chinese on their appointed course, but we could have gotten through to the Chinese people. Knowledge of a powerful protest would have penetrated and given the Chinese some grounds for believing they had not been entirely abandoned.

The U.S. teachers I met at the airport confirmed my belief that the students had been extremely fast in getting the truth out to the country. Word of Tiananmen had made it to Nanchang by Sunday afternoon, June 4, hours after the massacre. Protest demonstrations started immediately. Then students fanned out over the country to smaller towns, towns where they were not known. They walked up to people they had never seen before, delivered their message, and faded quickly into the background to find another ear. It was safer that way. They didn't know with whom they were talking and the person to whom they spoke did not know them. No trail for the secret police. Some believed the students' tale, some did not. But the students calculated that enough would know so that the seed was planted. As Mao said, a single spark can start a prairie fire. They didn't expect a prairie fire tomorrow, but the sparks were there, ready to be ignited when the moment was right.

School authorities were playing the government's game. All students have been ordered back to campus under threat of expulsion. Parents have been sent letters to persuade their sons and daughters to return. That will enable the secret police to interrogate them and discover whether they supported the protest movement. If a student doesn't show up within a week he is expelled, which automatically bars him from other institutions of higher learning.

■ Canton Airport, 3:00 P.M.

Met another American as we waited for baggage. He had been to Changsha. Very big demonstrations. But in countryside peasants didn't know what was going on. They had seen big crowds on Changsha streets. Didn't know what they were. Never had seen a demonstration. They were as ignorant of the world as in Mao's boyhood.

A Chinese student friend of this American's happened to be in Beijing during the June 4 weekend. He had gone to pick up his American visa to return to the United States. He was trapped near Tiananmen and spent the night on the streets. Nearly killed. He saw a Red Cross ambulance driver shot by PLA. (Was this the ambulance PLA showed on TV, claiming "bandits" shot the driver?) The Chinese student had heard PLA told ambulances not to pick up students — "Let them die." But ambulances paid no attention, picked up all the wounded. Not always the dead. No more room in hospitals.

Big demos in Chengdu and much fighting. Buildings burned.

The American student had heard that professors were sending their sons and daughters abroad, saying "Don't come back." That's what I began to hear early last fall. They *knew* it was coming.

The American had been tutoring two fifteen-year-old Chinese, a boy and a girl, in English. He carefully avoided political topics, but the girl asked him, "What happened at Tiananmen?" He said there had been a massacre of students. "But TV said only three students had been killed." He replied: "That's propaganda. Hundreds, maybe thousands were killed." The girl: "I don't know what to believe." The American: "Just keep your mind open and remember: Someday you will know the truth."

■ Canton, 10:00 P.M.

Staying at the White Swan. Luxurious. Stayed here just a year ago. Feels like Hong Kong, looks like Hong Kong, and it's empty — or almost so (30 percent occupied).

Almost out of China. Glad of it.

Had demos here but not so big. Good to get Hong Kong papers. Full of horror stories. Photos stained with blood of dead students. I had begun to feel relaxed. Then I read these horrors. It lies on my conscience. To think I know the men who did this!

Day Thirteen
June 13, 1989

■ Hong Kong, 3:30 P.M.

Out of China! Not really — Hong Kong is China.
But not formally until 1997, and I can't believe it will be
then. Not this fabulous, extraordinary creation of
Chinese and Western commercial talent. Not the world's
most flamboyant skyscrapers. Not millions of profit-
oriented, free Chinese. Not Hong Kong. Never. No matter what Margaret Thatcher says.

I'm going to take a shower and purge the dust of
China from my body.

■ Hong Kong, 4:30 P.M.

I'm sitting here looking out on Hong Kong Bay. Al-
most as I first saw it. We're in the new Victoria, down
Connaught Road a bit from the Mandarin, where
Charlotte and I first looked out on this jewel.

I've gotten the brown dust off my body but not the
ashes of Tiananmen out of my mind. Never will.

No problems at the Canton exit control. Waved us
right through. I hope the Tiananmen survivors got out as
easily. Afraid most of them will be picked up, turned in
by parents, relatives, friends, or themselves. China is so
big. But no escape.

I wish Charlotte were with me so we could look together on this city we saw together nearly twenty-five
years ago. Then we sailed the harbor with the Toppings

[Seymour, then the *New York Times* Hong Kong correspondent, and his wife, Audrey] on their junk. American destroyers, gray PRC gunboats with their gold-starred red flags, lazy P&O freighters, and thousands of little harbor craft. A traveler's delight. We did not know what went on behind the barbed wire of the Lo Wu frontier. We could only see grim PLA soldiers guarding the railroad bridge. We did not know the horrors of the Cultural Revolution. It was in full swing, cutting a swath so deep and broad in China's society that not a Chinese thought it could ever be repeated. They were wrong.

■ Hong Kong, 9:00 P.M.

A glorious Chinese meal. Too tired to enjoy it. Too tired to sort out all my impressions. But I have two or three things clear. Deng Xiaoping, whatever his physical state, is responsible. Yang Shangkun was chief of staff. The army carried out orders. The elders cheered. Zhao Ziyang went down in flames. The operation was planned long in advance. The shooting and the killing were not accidental. Deng Xiaoping wanted to "shed a little blood." He did. Like Lady Macbeth, he can scrub to eternity and he will never get the stain off his hands. Poor China.

A Fortnight Later

Back in Connecticut following Tiananmen and its aftermath. I think I have been able to fill out the story of the massacre — how it happened, why it happened, who was responsible, and what lies ahead.

It is not a pretty tale. The origins go back to the autumn of 1986 and the vicious campaign that drove out Hu Yaobang, with his brilliant, almost childlike curiosity and daring ideas. Hu was a man intent on real change in China. He had Deng's confidence. He was a genuine threat to the geriatric relics of the Long March and to their reactionary allies, the military.

Like Deng, Hu had little sense of measure. He often overshot the mark. It may seem silly, but his off-the-cuff proposal that China abandon chopsticks in favor of Western knives and forks was the straw that broke the camel's back.

All of China hooted Hu down. Much of the West joined in. This and a dozen similar eccentricities were picked upon by the elders when Hu demonstrated sympathy and an inability (or unwillingness) to combat student and intellectual unrest. The student pro-democracy demonstrations began in the fall of 1986 and peaked in November and December.

Hu tendered his resignation as party secretary on January 16, 1987. Almost immediately a campaign against what was called spiritual pollution was launched, designed to combat the Western ideas that Hu had permitted to flourish. Liu Binyan, China's most influential newspaper writer, an investigative reporter of heroic stature, was expelled from the Communist party and forbidden to write for his newspaper, the *People's Daily*. Liu specialized in exposés of corruption within the Communist party, particularly in the provinces. He was hated by party politicians for his honesty and courage. He proclaimed himself — much as did the students on Tiananmen — as a supporter of an ethical Communism, one true to its ideals and not dedicated to privilege and power.

This was the public side of the Hu Yaobang–"spiritual pollution" crisis.

There was a hidden agenda, as I discovered in following up the revelation that PLA officers at that time were forbidden to listen to BBC and VOA.

The army and public security administration began, for the first time, to prepare for riot control. Both the army and the Security Bureau purchased riot-control equipment, including tear gas, other crowd-control chemicals, stanchions, and protective clothing for the riot force. Selected military and security battalions, including the elite 8341 regiment stationed in Zhongnanhai, began training in crowd control.

The security forces probably began to study South Korean tactics in combating student demonstrations. The Security Bureau purchased a device that went into extensive use in the Tiananmen crisis, a miniature TV camera developed by the Japanese that is smaller than an electric pencil sharpener. The camera can be automatically controlled from a central station to transmit pictures of all four sides of an intersection. The Japanese used the images from these cameras to help adjust the stop-and-go system of traffic lights, to speed the flow of traffic through congested areas. The Chinese purchased seventy-three of these cameras and put them up at Beijing's principal intersections. They said they would use them to spot traffic violators. The videotape pictures taken by the cameras would provide irrefutable evidence of violations.

Whether that innocent purpose was the real reason behind the purchase cannot be known. In fact, in the Tiananmen affair the cameras were used to photograph demonstrators, street battles, and students. They produced grainy, low-lighting pictures seen by American (and Chinese) viewers on TV of many of the combat actions. These cameras enabled the Security Bureau to identify participants in the demonstrations.

But there is no evidence that the troops brought into the city had had the benefit of the special riot training. The evidence goes the other way. On July 2 Li Peng told an American-Chinese visitor that the army had been compelled to use live bullets because it possessed neither tear gas nor rubber bullets. But tear gas *was* employed by some units, including the 8341 regiment. If riot-control equipment was not on hand, it could readily have been purchased and delivered in the six weeks between the decision to use force and June 4. Clearly, the government wanted a riot — a police riot.

The fact that these preparations were put in motion in early 1987, a time when student demonstrations were more intense than they had been at any time since Deng Xiaoping came to power, supports my notion that the military was readying itself for another and more severe outbreak of unrest.

There was no way in advance to predict that Hu Yaobang would die on April 15, 1989, nor that his death would touch off escalating student demonstrations.

There had been a spate of rumors in March and early April of 1989 of a possible comeback for Hu. Much attention was given to an unusual photograph published by the Beijing papers of him and Zhao Ziyang in friendly conversation. Hu had been suffering from heart disease but was said to be in improved health. However, he suffered a massive heart attack at a Politburo meeting on April 8, brought on, some said, by a violent disagreement over educational policy and, quite possibly, over the government's attitude toward the students. The report of a violent quarrel in the Politburo was officially denied.

Hu's death touched off immediate demonstrations at Beijing and other universities, rapidly snowballing into marches on Tiananmen Square.

This was the kind of disturbance that the security officials had had in mind when they embarked on their preparations. It is probable that the crisis they envisioned was the inevitable emergency that would accompany the death of Deng Xiaoping. "Plan A" was likely drafted for this event. When the Hu Yaobang demonstrations escalated and the decision was made on April 26 to employ force (reflected in a *People's Daily* editorial of that date), Plan A was apparently put into place as a method of dealing with the Tiananmen contingency.

That Deng Xiaoping was directly involved in this there is no doubt. A variety of sources attest that he took part in the deliberations and that, at some point, he became convinced that a plot threatening not only to overthrow the party but also to take his life and those of other leaders was developing under cover of the student protests.

Deng, having come to power after the chaos, paranoia, intrigue, and plots of the Cultural Revolution and the Gang of Four, was highly sensitive to such dangers. He had not returned to the elite compound of Zhongnanhai when he came to power in 1977–78, and he discouraged his associates from living there. "It is not safe," he said: "one bomb could kill us all." He had a house built for himself with stringent security features, TV monitors, steel walls, bullet-proof glass. It is located just north of the Forbidden City, adjacent to the Defense Ministry, in Iron Lion Lane, where the old imperial granaries once stood.

One of Deng's first moves as the Tiananmen crisis mounted was to change the palace guards (his personal guards, that is), and he instructed his associates to take the same precaution. This was a page out of Stalin's book. The Soviet dictator periodically changed his personal guards and usually had them shot. He acted on the theory that after a few years in a position of high trust a man inevitably would be tempted to join the other side. If he hadn't — too bad. Stalin was taking no chances. Neither was Deng. (The changing of guards had also been a frequent tactic of Mao's and of Jiang Qing's and her Gang of Four.)

Whether at this time Deng moved out of his bullet-proof house to the security of a special nuclear-safe command center in the military district of the Fragrant Hills, to the west, is not certain. But at a key point in the developing drama Deng and his closest colleagues did move there to direct operations.

Amid these mounting tensions Party Secretary Zhao Ziyang departed for North Korea on a state visit, leaving Beijing by special train on April 23. Three days later, in his absence, the decision was made to employ military force against the demonstrators but to delay action until after the Gorbachev visit, May 15–17. The text of the *People's Daily* editorial reflecting that decision was telegraphed to Zhao in Pyongyang. Zhao, so I have been told, concurred in it. The rationales were the growing chaos in the city, the need to restore party discipline, the rising impact on industrial production, and (supposed) evidence that a plot against the government was taking shape.

Zhao got back to Beijing on April 30. The crisis had heightened. The students were planning a huge protest for May 4, anniversary of the 1919 demonstration. Zhao found himself selected to give a milk-and-waterish May 4 speech, and he received firsthand information from his own staff about the true nature of the demonstrations.

Serious doubts arose in Zhao's mind about the hardline solution. At the initiative of the Military Commission, troop movements were already under way. Deng was chairman of the Military Commission, Zhao vice chairman, and Yang Shangkun permanent vice-chairman, nominally number three on the organizational chart but, in fact, operating head of the body. (Deng has often insisted that Zhao was concentrating on the work of the Military Commission, but it is doubtful that this was true.)

The Military Commission occupies a unique position in China. Because the Red Army under Mao brought about the Revolution, the commission has always had a special place. Mao served as commision chairman during his life. Deng has held that post while ostensibly shedding all others. It is the supreme and ultimate authority in China.

In Zhao's absence, plans for the military solution of Tiananmen had gone forward swiftly under Yang Shangkun's direction. Zhao was not without influence with the military; he had close ties with the defense minister, former commander of the Beijing military district, and some other professional military men. But, of course, Deng had been put into office by a group of old Long March commanders, some of whom in retirement still commanded enormous prestige, both military and political. The weight of Deng and Yang Shangkun outbalanced that of Zhao in a ratio of 100 to 1.

With the troops already moving in and the visit of Gorbachev days away, Zhao shifted his position. He decided to oppose a military solution. His decision aroused anger and dismay. "But you had agreed to the proposal," he was told. "How can you change your mind?"

Zhao held his ground. He could not be party to the planned action. Zhao's stand threw the leadership into confusion. At all costs it wanted to present a united front. The row raged right into the Gorbachev visit. Zhao tried to resolve the matter by tendering his resignation. That was refused, just as Liu Shaoqi's had been during the Cultural Revolution. Liu had gone to Zhou Enlai and admitted that he had made mistakes; Mao had pointed them out. He wanted to resign, go back to a farm in Yanan, and retire. He would take all responsibility on himself — it was his fault, not that of his associates. Let him quit and let the country get on with its business. Zhou Enlai

163

replied sadly: "I am sorry but you will not be permitted to resign."

Zhao took his case to Yang Shangkun, who had become very close to him. Several times in difficult periods Yang had been of assistance. Zhao told Yang that he had to see Deng Xiaoping and put his case before him. Yang pondered a moment and then, it was said, told Zhao: "I'm sorry. But in this case I can't help you." Yang had become Deng's gatekeeper.

Zhao took a bold step. He told Yang he, too, was sorry, but he could not support a decision with which he did not agree.

It may have been this defiance of the party line that emboldened Zhao to tell Mikhail Gorbachev that while Deng had given up all his positions at the 1987 Thirteenth Party Congress, he had actually retained a veto over everything. "We agreed," said Zhao, "to submit all important questions to him."

This was hardly news. It had been apparent to all that regardless of title, Deng possessed the highest authority in the country. But Zhao's honest acknowledgment of this universally known secret sealed his fate.

Not only was Zhao refusing to accept a party decision, he was telling the head of China's great and sometimes hostile neighbor a party "secret."

Events raced forward. Gorbachev came and went. Hardly had the Soviet leader left town than on May 18 Deng left as well. He went to Wuhan, where he had, as chairman of the Military Commission, convened a meeting of the heads of China's seven military districts. He had summoned the commanders to extract from them a pledge of support for the military crackdown at

Tiananmen. He spent the day with the commanders and came away with their unanimous support in hand. The way was cleared for action.

On May 19 Zhao visited the student hunger strikers at Tiananmen. He had fought for three days for permission to go there. Finally, the party leaders gave in. Zhao went, but he was accompanied by an unsmiling, laconic Li Peng. With tears in his eyes, Zhao spoke to the hunger strikers. He said he had come "too late, too late" but expressed hope that the students' high aspirations ultimately would be met. Li Peng said nothing. Later that evening under Li's signature and that of Yang Shangkun the order placing Tiananmen and other areas of Beijing under martial law was issued.

Tragedy now waited around the corner.

Why had events reached this critical point? There were two possible causes. First, Deng felt — and declared to his party associates — that Zhao had betrayed him, specifically by the remark to Gorbachev, and in general by his support of the students and refusal to follow the party diktat. It is not clear that Deng believed Zhao was engaged in a conspiracy, but it is clear that there were those who were making such suggestions to Deng. For Deng, Zhao's "betrayal" may have served as the final impetus to go ahead with the crackdown, an action that had been delayed several times to that point — probably by Deng himself, against the desires of the hard-liners on the Standing Committee.

Second, from the earliest days of his comeback Deng held a negative attitude toward the students. He and his fellow members in what was simply called the club, a cozy institution where Deng and his council of elders met to gossip, to plan, and to play bridge, contemptuously termed the young *wa wa,* children. They were uppity, rambunctious, ungrateful. They didn't know their place. The elders knew best. The wa wa did not appreciate what had been done for them. As Deng told his fellow club members, he had given them more presents than anyone else who had ruled China. He let them go abroad by the tens of thousands to study or to work. He put no impediment on what they read or wrote (hardly true). The state was spending more money than ever to educate them. The state had treated them like prodigal children — and how had they repaid this?

With shouts and slogans and, worst of all, with total betrayal. At a time when he was engaged in the supreme diplomatic negotiations of his career, those with Mikhail Gorbachev, they had publicly humiliated him. They had caused him to disrupt his schedule of meetings and entertainment. He did not know from one moment to another where he could meet his guest; he was no longer master in his own house. This had never happened in history to a chief of state. "I could not figure out who was in charge," Gorbachev was quoted as saying after his Beijing visit.

Deng put his relationship to Zhao and to the students in the same context — they had both caused him loss of face and personal humiliation. As one who knows Deng well told me: Deng is a brilliant man, brave, courageous, bold. He took the steps that had to be taken to get the country going after Mao and the Gang of Four. But he has a terrible weakness. If he thinks someone he trusts has let him down or betrayed him, his temper is like lightning. Nothing can withstand him. This is the great tragedy.

I think, however, that Deng's temper is not the whole answer. I date the problem back a year, just as I was leaving China at the end of June 1988. I had expected to meet with Deng, and this hope had been encouraged by Yang Shangkun, who was my liaison with Deng — but the meeting never materialized. Deng had gone to Beidaihe, his usual summer retreat. He swam and relaxed there each year, and the government moved there, too.

That June 1988 the party simply split apart. As it met at Beidaihe, it was unable to agree on how to handle urgent problems. Basically those were economic — the uneven pace of development, the overinvestment in non-economic high-rise office buildings and hotels, the uncontrolled pouring of state funds into trivial municipal and county projects, often riddled with graft, the inability of banks and fiscal controllers to curb racing inflation and the rise of the cost of living.

Two things made it impossible to resolve these issues: Deng's insistence that his development program move forward in the fast lane, and the savage attack of the party reactionaries, who sensed a strategic moment to dump the whole Deng program.

Aided by some of the military, the elders succeeded better than perhaps even they realized. They halted the Deng program. Decisions were postponed until a later meeting, in July, when Deng was compelled to accept transfer of economic questions from Zhao's hands to those of Premier Li Peng. To protect Deng — beginning now to show age-slowed responses — blame for the troubles was heaped on Zhao (just as earlier, in 1986–87, it had been heaped on Hu Yaobang).

The Beidaihe meetings resolved nothing. The crisis continued. The government allotted token subsidies to the hard-pinched Beijingers and other big-city residents. The question of graft and corruption and influence peddling by sons, daughters, and relatives got only lip service.

The arguments at Beidaihe were no more effective than those in Petrograd in 1916 and early 1917, when Czar Nicholas II and his advisers struggled to resolve the crisis that was overwhelming Russia. They changed nothing but the names of the ministers.

China rolled ahead to disaster with the players in the power elite worrying not about the country but about how the power pie would be cut. The oligarchs saw a chance to prolong their reign a few more years. The military knew it held the top cards and that in a crisis power would flow its way. Some individuals, like Yang Shangkun, saw a chance for a quantum leap upward.

What Deng thought or felt is not recorded.

In August 1988, just after the events at Beidaihe, I met a gifted (but sometimes mistaken) observer of the Chinese political scene. He had been in China and was in a state of great excitement. Deng had lost control. He was no longer in charge. He thought everything must be done immediately — while he was still among the living. Haste was the only word he understood. He was not in touch with reality. He no longer was able to judge a situation on the basis of real evidence. No one could talk to him. The sessions at Beidaihe had been a failure. They had broken up with everyone in conflict. The countryside was in awful shape. No food. The cities were a disaster because of inflation. No meat in city or country. A total mess. The slogan was going around: "Better Mao and 48 than Deng and 108" — meaning that earning 48 yuan a month under Mao was better than earning 108 yuan under Deng.

I was appalled. This report did not jibe with anything I had seen. I knew it was false in major segments: The countryside was not starving. There was plenty of food and plenty of money. I had been traveling in China almost continuously for six or seven months. This was not a description of the China I knew.

What bothered me most was that this description was issuing from very high quarters, from persons who had been at Beidaihe. This might not be the true situation, but it was the situation in which they wanted others to believe.

I was so upset by the report that I wrote some of my highly placed Chinese contacts and told them they should know what kind of stories were emerging from official quarters in China. I thought it was propaganda to support the campaign of the reactionaries to drive Zhao from office and compel Deng to abandon his Reform and Opening policies. In so doing China would move back toward the bankruptcy of Stalinist economics — just at a time when the Soviets were trying to imitate China's remarkable innovations.

I smelled high politics — succession politics — in all this. The struggle for the dragon throne was under way. It seemed likely that Deng was losing vigor. Possibly he was getting out of touch. Possibly there were those in whose interest it was to detach Deng from reality. Much the same had happened in Mao's last years.

After this I watched closely and listened to my Chinese friends. The battle swirled around Zhao. Sometimes the liberals seemed to gain a bit, sometimes Zhao unexpectedly emerged into prominence, then was lost in a swirl of political fog. Li Peng's picture moved in and out of circulation. A political battle was in progress, but it was hard to distinguish it from the normal give-and-take of Chinese politics.

Certainly I had no premonition, as China moved toward the fortieth anniversary of the Communist Revolution and the tenth year of the Deng regime, that she would explode into Tiananmen.

Nor did the emergence of the student demonstrations in April 1989 and their escalation into May and finally June seem to me to presage disaster. I confess I was mystified at the irresolution of the government and its unwillingness to enter into a simple dialogue with the students at an early stage, when an easy solution was not beyond reach.

As tension rose, as the troops moved in, as the government began to prepare for arbitrary action, another suspicion arose. Was there not something deliberate in all this? Was the crisis temperature being allowed to rise until military action became inevitable and even necessary?

That hypothesis becomes inescapable when viewed against the background of the government's program. It was — and is — totally unable to cope with the economic problems that have been spun off by Deng's fast-paced development. Nor does it seem able or willing to touch the issue of graft in high places. This made more attractive a military solution. It would solve nothing basic, but it would terrorize the population and give the party a chance to impose absolute control on an unruly citizenry. It would keep them from shouting. They might suffer and starve, but they would be afraid of the army's guns. Harsh, yes. But to preserve its power, the junta would halt at nothing. The notion, held by many Americans, that the bright young people in Tiananmen were touching the hearts and minds of Deng and his men was naive.

Unless the army was a complete society of fools, only a deliberate desire to initiate and continue terror could explain the manner in which Tiananmen was handled — the extraordinary firepower directed at random against the citizenry. Whatever the number of students killed on Tiananmen, it was only a fraction of the general public mowed down.

The incredulity over the casualty figures of three or four thousand reflected the fact that these casualties were not inflicted in the center of town but in the outskirts, where the conduct of the PLA had touched off a genuine people's war. Tens and hundreds of thousands of ordinary citizens sprang from houses and flats to oppose armor with bare hands. The spectacle of the lone man dancing in front of an armored column to bring it to a halt was a symbol of the people of Beijing. They emerged en masse to try to convince the people's army that they were the people.

A man of whom I heard walked from the suburbs and up to the barrier line just beyond the Beijing Hotel early on the evening of June 4. He walked to that point and the Tiananmen troops opened fire. The bullets coursed past him on either side. He could not believe it. He threw himself on the pavement, arms outstretched. A bullet hit a foot ahead of him, spattering fragments that injured his hand. He went to the Capitol hospital, where his wound was treated after a long wait. They had many more serious cases. Doctors in some hospitals operated for seventy-two hours without halt. Many deaths resulted when blood supplies ran out.

Why did you go to Tiananmen? the man was asked.

"I had to tell them," he said. "I had to talk to them and tell them that *we* were the people."

No one who saw or talked to the people of Beijing can believe that they will easily swallow the government line that Tiananmen did not happen, that only "bad men" and "bandits" burned the trucks and held back the troops.

To the people of Beijing it is apparent that the mantle of heaven, which slipped from the death grasp of Mao Zedong to the agile hands of Deng Xiaoping, has slipped once again. Deng has lost it and no one yet has retrieved it.

And what of the future? I have heard estimates of six months to two years before there is another shuffle of the deck. That depends on the lives of elderly men, particularly the life of Deng Xiaoping. His mind, I have been told, is clear, if not as nimble as it was. His body has deteriorated this last year. The process is irreversible. Hopefully he will not sink into the vegetative state in which Mao spent his last years, totally manipulated by unscrupulous handlers.

Already it is said that Deng is much in the control of a small band of individuals. He spends little time on affairs of state (is not strong enough or lacks the will), accepts the evaluations of others, has little firsthand knowledge of conditions, is totally unaware of the reality of Tiananmen, quite possibly believes the vapid propaganda of the army and the party.

Deng's speech of June 9 to the military commanders, congratulating them on their actions of June 4, was read abroad as bristling with anger and the determination to use any means necessary to regain control of the "counterrevolutionary" situation.

So Deng said, but the full text of the speech discloses a baffled, almost bewildered old man, painfully clutching at his vision of a new, open, and reformed China, a China that will go forward to economic vigor and meet his goals for the year 2050. It is apologetic in tone. Deng is obviously stunned at the resistance the people put up to the PLA crackdown. There is a plaintive vein of incomprehension running through his remarks, as though he cannot really believe it all happened, that his dreams and ambitions have been shattered in a single tragic night.

There is no way that Deng's condition will take a turn for the better. The trend is down and it will not change. Yang Shangkun has acquired enormous influence with Deng, with the army, and with the elders. But although more vigorous than Deng, he is only two years his junior. He too has entered a zone in which physical and mental frailty may readily make their appearance. And he is not without enemics. He did not receive a unanimous vote in his election to the Military Commission.

None of my Chinese friends believes Li Peng has a constituency. They see him as an instrument, not a player. They do not expect his power to grow. The new party secretary, Zhang Ziemin, has no wide political base. He has only Shanghai behind him, and even there he is not too popular. This is hardly an accident. When Mao had to pick a successor after the death of Zhou Enlai and the second fall of Deng Xiaopong, he picked Hua Guofeng, a political unknown whom he had met in his native Hunan. He didn't want a man of power. Deng's choice of Zhang was based on the same kind of political calculation. With Li and Zhang in place Deng feels no political threat.

It is a situation pleasing to the army. The military has demonstrated to Deng that without it he cannot retain power. The commanders have demonstrated to themselves that they are more powerful than Deng or the party. On the next round they expect to pick their man for the top office. Not necessarily an army man, but one who can head a tightly run military state. Something, say, like South Korea. With a doctrine that has already been evolved by the reactionaries, a doctrine called authoritarianism (which is just what it says, a gloss of Nazism and fascism), they think they can do very well. Who needs democracy? The fast-moving Asian "tigers" have done very well without democracy. China, they think, is too big, too inchoate to function under such a system. With authoritarianism, some pleasant graft, and the guns of the armored divisions China should do very well.

As I have been writing these lines I have talked to some of my Chinese friends. What is there to hope for? They shake their heads in despair. "This is only the beginning," they say. They think of it in terms of the unthinkable: the Cultural Revolution in reruns, China sinking back into the sloth of warlordism, fascism.

I fear they are right. I confess I was one who thought the students in Tiananmen could change the mind of the stubborn men who run the country. Yes, even that of Deng Xiaoping.

I was as naive as that young man from Nankai whom I met in the square. I thought he and his comrades were the wave of the future. Like so many Americans, I was very proud of the youngsters, so brave, so idealistic.

Now I know that China is still ruled by her three great symbols: the Yellow River, the Great Wall, and the Dragon. The Yellow River is believed to have given birth to Chinese civilization thousands of years ago in its rich alluvial soil and to have established China as a river country, not an ocean country. She still lives by the yellow river waters, not the blue of ocean seas, turning inward instead of outward, as did the men of the Renaissance and the privateers of Queen Elizabeth. Not yet have the people and their rulers begun to see that the Great Wall keeps the people in, as well as invaders out; that the walls and courtyards in which they contain themselves, the great magenta walls that surround the Forbidden City and Zhongnanhai, confine minds as well as bodies. And the Dragon is still supreme, China's benevolent dragon that protects the nation, protects the throne, protects the dynasties, protects the people — so long as they do not threaten its order.

Now I know that these myths still hold China under their sway. The TV documentary *Yellow River Elegy,* which challenged them, has not torn China away from her ancient foundations. "If they had only discussed these ideas," said the director of the documentary the night before the guns roared at Tiananmen, "they would not be in this situation."

He was right, but now, I am afraid, it will be years before the bright dreams of the *Elegy* will gleam through the dark clouds of the Dragon, break down the barrier of the Great Wall, and send China soaring away from the silt of the Yellow River into the clean blue waters of the sea and the endless precincts of space.